India and South Africa

South Africa and India constitute two key nodes in the global south and have inspired new modes of non-Western transnational history. Themes include anti-imperial movements; Gandhian ideas; comparisons of race and caste; Afro-Asian ideals; and Indian Ocean public spheres. This volume extends these debates into the cultural and linguistic terrain. The book combines the methods of Indian Ocean studies and Comparative Cultural Studies, both committed to moving beyond the nation state. Case studies explore classics and concomitant ideas of civilisation, colonial linguistics and the history of languages, and theatre. Topics include the use of classics by colonisers and the colonised in British India and South Africa; differences between South African Indian English and Indian English; how the Linguistic Survey of India conflicted with colonial and nationalist mappings of India and its references to African languages; the rise of 'Hinglish' in contemporary India; a South African play dealing with African-Indian interactions. This book was published as a special issue of *African Studies*.

Javed Majeed is Professor of English and Comparative Literature at King's College, London. He is currently writing a monograph on Grierson's Linguistic Survey of India. His previous publications include *Autobiography, Travel and Postnational Identity* (2007, Indian edition 2014), *Muhammad Iqbal: Islam, Aesthetics, and Postcolonialism* (2009), and *James Mill's The History of British India and Orientalism* (1992).

Isabel Hofmeyr is Professor of African Literature at the University of the Witwatersrand. She is also Global Distinguished Professor at NYU. Her recent books include *Gandhi's Printing Press: Experiments in Slow Reading* (2013) and a collection of essays *Ten Books that Shaped the British Empire: Shaping an Imperial Commons* (2014), edited with Antoinette Burton.

India and South Africa

Edited by
Javed Majeed and Isabel Hofmeyr

Routledge
Taylor & Francis Group
LONDON AND NEW YORK

First published 2016 by Routledge

2 Park Square, Milton Park, Abingdon, Oxfordshire OX14 4RN
711 Third Avenue, New York, NY 10017

Routledge is an imprint of the Taylor & Francis Group, an informa business

First issued in paperback 2017

British Library Cataloguing in Publication Data
A catalogue record for this book is available from the British Library

ISBN 13: 978-1-138-18283-7 (hbk)
ISBN 13: 978-1-138-50248-2 (pbk)

Typeset in Times New Roman
by RefineCatch Limited, Bungay, Suffolk

Publisher's Note
The publisher accepts responsibility for any inconsistencies that may have arisen during the conversion of this book from journal articles to book chapters, namely the possible inclusion of journal terminology.

Contents

Citation Information

The chapters in this book were originally published in *African Studies*, volume 74, issue 2 (August 2015). When citing this material, please use the original page numbering for each article, as follows:

Chapter 1
Introduction: India and South Africa – Comparisons, Confluences, Contrasts
Javed Majeed and Isabel Hofmeyr
African Studies, volume 74, issue 2 (August 2015) pp 149–156

Chapter 2
Gandhi, Carpenter, Schreiner and the Crisis of Modern Civilisation at the Turn of the 20th Century
John Hilton
African Studies, volume 74, issue 2 (August 2015) pp 157–174

Chapter 3
Gandhi and Socrates
Phiroze Vasunia
African Studies, volume 74, issue 2 (August 2015) pp 175–185

Chapter 4
English in India and South Africa: Comparisons, Commonalities and Contrasts
Rajend Mesthrie
African Studies, volume 74, issue 2 (August 2015) pp 186–198

Chapter 5
Dil Maange More*: Cultural Contexts of Hinglish in Contemporary India*
Francesca Orsini
African Studies, volume 74, issue 2 (August 2015) pp 199–220

Chapter 6
'A State of Affairs which is Essentially Indefinite': The Linguistic Survey of India (1894–1927)
Javed Majeed
African Studies, volume 74, issue 2 (August 2015) pp 221–234

Chapter 7

Performing History and Constructing 'Culture': Ronnie Govender's 1949 *and the Romanticism of Historical Memory*
Neilesh Bose
African Studies, volume 74, issue 2 (August 2015) pp 235–246

Notes on Contributors

Neilesh Bose is a professor at the University of Victoria, Canada, and a historian of modern South Asia, cultural and intellectual history, diasporas and migrations, and the history and politics of theatre and performance. His books include *Beyond Bollywood and Broadway: Plays from the South Asian Diaspora* (2009), *Recasting Region: Language, Culture, and Islam in Colonial Bengal* (2014), and *Culture and Power in South Asian Islam: Defying the Perpetual Exception* (2015).

John Hilton is Professor of Classics at the University of KwaZulu-Natal, Howard College, Durban, South Africa. He was awarded his doctorate – a philological commentary on Books 3 and 4 of the Aethiopica of Heliodorus – by the University of Natal in 1998. He has contributed to studies in Classical Reception Theory and numerous chapters and articles on various topics, with particular reference to slavery at the Cape of Good Hope, the ancient novel (especially *Heliodorus*), onomastics (the name Azania and the names given to the nations of Africa), classical reception studies, and computer applications in classical philology. He is currently editor of *Acta Classica: Proceedings of the Classical Association of South Africa.*

Isabel Hofmeyr is Professor of African Literature at the University of the Witwatersrand. She is also Global Distinguished Professor at NYU. Her recent books include *Gandhi's Printing Press: Experiments in Slow Reading* (2013) and a collection of essays *Ten Books that Shaped the British Empire: Shaping an Imperial Commons* (2014), edited with Antoinette Burton.

Javed Majeed is Professor of English and Comparative Literature at King's College, London. He is currently writing a monograph on Grierson's Linguistic Survey of India. His previous publications include *Autobiography, Travel and Postnational Identity* (2007, Indian edition 2014), *Muhammad Iqbal: Islam, Aesthetics, and Postcolonialism* (2009), and *James Mill's The History of British India and Orientalism* (1992).

Rajend Mesthrie is Professor of Linguistics at the University of Cape Town in the School of African & Gender Studies, Linguistics & Anthropology. He holds an NRF research chair in Migration, Language and Social Change. Among his publications are *Language in South Africa* (2002), *World Englishes* (2008), and *A Dictionary of South African Indian English* (2012).

Francesca Orsini is Professor of Hindi and South Asian Literature at the University of London. Her PhD research at SOAS was on the Hindi public sphere of the 1920s and

1930s, published as *The Hindi Public Sphere 1920–1940: Language and Literature in the Age of Nationalism* (2002). She joined SOAS in 2006, where she teaches courses on Hindi language, literature, the literary history of South Asia, and contemporary politics of culture.

Phiroze Vasunia is Professor of Greek at University College London. He is the author of *The Classics and Colonial India* (2013), among other publications.

Introduction: India and South Africa – Comparisons, Confluences, Contrasts

Javed Majeed and Isabel Hofmeyr

King's College London and University of the Witwatersrand

The articles in this Special Issue come out of papers delivered at a conference called 'India and South Africa: comparisons, confluences, contrasts', organised by Javed Majeed and held at King's College London in October 2012.[1] The aim of the conference was to deepen the interdisciplinary nature of literary studies (especially in its comparative literary dimensions) and Indian Ocean studies by building links between these two areas. From its inception in the 19th century up to the present day the practices and theories of Comparative Literature have, of course, been critical of nationally defined literary canons, and one of its defining aims continues to be transnational readings of literature and literary history. Scholars in Indian Ocean studies have also stressed how their work on transnationalism challenges nationally-based historiographies. In addition, academics in both fields have re-thought the category of 'Area Studies', either by moving away from what they see as its constraining legacies, or by appropriating its linguistic and textual expertise in new configurations within a more thoroughly globalised Comparative Literature (Hofmeyr & Williams 2011; Bose 2006:chapter 1; Spivak 2004; Saussy 2006). The conference therefore aimed to create a space for further transnational revisions of 'Area Studies' and nationalism in both fields by bringing together their different methodologies.

Comparative and connective work on India and South Africa has generated a long historiographical tradition. Its earlier instantiations focused on indentured labour and 'passenger' Indians, largely merchants following in the wake of indentured workers. Mohandas Gandhi and his political mobilisations constituted another important focus. In keeping with earlier historiographies of diasporic communities, this body of work was often narrowly ethnicised (focusing only on 'Indians' and excluding other groups from the frame) and tended to have a 'one-way' orientation, namely it only tracked movement in one direction from South Asia to Africa without looking at reverse movement or asking what the implications of this migration were back home (Dhupelia-Mesthrie 2007). The transnational turn and the move beyond nation and area as units of analysis have opened up this field considerably. Studies of 'Indian' communities have been de-ethnicised with other communities being brought into the picture.

There has also been a focus on southern African Indians (and others) who travel into the Indian Ocean world whether itinerant merchants (Vahed 2005; Dhupelia-Mesthrie 2012), Mozambican Goans (Gupta 2007), South African political exiles in India, or African Protestants who visited India on ecumenical networks (Erlank 2009). Another productive line of enquiry has been to examine the meanings of 'Africa' in India whether through the reception of the Anglo-Boer War in India (Datta 2007) or through studies of African communities in India or through the semi-colonial perceptions of Africa as the 'dark continent' that remain current in some parts of Indian public life (Hofmeyr 2007; Burton 2012). These various themes have seeped into a number of disciplinary areas: these include global labour history where the porous boundaries between slavery, abolition, indenture, forced labour, and 'free' labour have come to constitute an important site for thinking about unfree labour and the evolution of capitalism (Anderson 2012; Stanziani 2014); studies of South Asian global migration and the ways in which these shape the making of colonial boundaries and ideas of sovereignty and citizenship (Dhupelia-Mesthrie 2014; Macdonald 2012; McKeown 2008); southern African political history where the shifting boundaries between 'African' and 'Indian' has helped revise the dominant narrative of South Africa as solely a story of struggle between 'black' and 'white' (Soske 2009). These various studies have demonstrated South Africa as a space of configuration and triangulation, a post-area studies zone in which different 'areas' (South Asia, Africa, China etc) interact through the various migrant communities that were extruded into the region.

While taking cognisance of this work, we wanted to address the role comparativism has played in the development of a number of academic disciplines as they relate to southern Africa and India during the colonial and postcolonial periods, including linguistics, literature, jurisprudence and politics. The conference garnered some interesting papers addressing such topics as the biopolitics of caste and race, the inception and writing of the constitutions of both nation-states, the history and varieties of English in southern Africa and India, the linguistic mapping of India and southern Africa in the colonial period and its legacies, and the role of classics in imperial pedagogy and its legacies in both societies. The conference also had a session on the role of theatre in representing, mediating and resolving conflict which included readings by Mahesh Dattani and Craig Higginson from their plays.

The exploration of these topics helped us to develop the themes and practices of cross-regional comparisons in the global South. In the end, though, because of participants' commitments, the papers we received for publication fell into the areas of linguistics and the history of languages, classics and concomitant ideas of civilisation, and theatre.

Civilisational discourse was of course central to European colonial ideologies in the age of imperialism, and was defined and honed in overlapping and contrasting ways in colonial India and southern Africa. Like the category of religion, civilisation and what it consisted of was thought and re-thought, interrogated and re-affirmed, subverted and reinforced in novels, pamphlets and many other genres of writing, not to mention painting. Symptomatic of this struggle over the meaning of the category and history of 'civilisation' is of course Mahatma Gandhi's *Hind Swaraj* (1909) with its systematic exploration and even inversion of the term in chapter 6. The fact that Gandhi felt it necessary to address the issue reflects the key character of this concept. While anti-colonial nationalism worked with ideas of bordered territoriality, it nonetheless often grounded itself in civilisational discourses which by their very nature extend beyond the boundaries of the nation-state. The complex relationship between the idea of a bounded nation and the larger civilisational identities which transcend it was also explored in Rabindranath Tagore's interesting essays in *Greater India* (1921) and Jawaharlal Nehru in his *Discovery of India* (1946); both reflect upon the history of Indian civilisation extending to the region of South East Asia in terms of architecture, Sanskrit literature, religion, art and other cultural forms of expression and its significance for India as a bounded territory.

In colonial India Graeco-Roman notions of civilisation informed British imperial sensibilities (Vasunia 2013).[2] In the early period of established British rule in India, the famous linguist and legal scholar Sir William Jones (1746–1794) compared the deities of ancient Rome and Greece to those of India, and in the context of his proposed digest of Indian laws, described himself as the 'Justinian of India' (Majeed 1992:chapter 1). Comparisons with the Roman Empire also formed an important part of British imperial self-definitions. In works such as CP Lucas's *Greater Rome and Greater Britain* (1912) and James Bryce's *The Ancient Roman Empire and the British Empire in India. The Diffusion of Roman and English Law throughout the World* (1914) these comparisons tended to cluster around problematic areas of race and identity, in which allusions to Rome were anxious rather than reinforcing (Majeed 1999). European classical learning also played a key role in the syllabi for the Indian Civil Service examinations where the scheme of marking and the reading lists reflected the importance given to this learning in shaping the class and gender identities of imperial administrators for India (Majeed 1999; Vasunia 2013:chapter 5).

Both colonisers and the colonised in British India engaged with ideas of Graeco-Roman antiquity in order to make new cross-cultural connections and to articulate the conditions and historical experiences that they were grappling with (Vasunia 2013:27–8). By the 1850s, Indian and other Asian intellectuals' understanding of the ancient and medieval history of southern Asia had formulated into an influential pattern, in which comparisons of ancient India with Greece and Rome were important in their writings (Bayly 2011:47, 163ff). Urdu poets like Altaf Husain Hali (1837–1914) and Muhammad Iqbal (1877–1938) used ancient Greece and Rome as tropes for a variety of purposes in their poems, while both Gandhi and Nehru re-presented Plato and Socrates (and ancient Greece as whole) within their differing versions of Indian nationalism (Majeed 2006, 2007:chapter 7; Vasunia 2013:335–49). Alongside a transnational,

Indian-inflected Hellenism, elaborate comparisons between ancient India, Rome and Greece were also a prominent strand in the political and historical works of Indian liberal thinkers in the 19th and 20th centuries (Bayly 2011:180, 189; Vasunia 2013:122).

The uses of classical civilisation in South Africa were both similar and different, created by a rich and variegated traditions of classical thinking which worked both with and against imperialism. As John Hilton (2007) has argued, European colonial ideas drew on classical templates in a variety of ways which included the naming of regions of the continent via Graeco-Roman vectors (Azania in *Periplus Maris Erthyraei*); Luis Vaz de Camões' Homeric and Vergilian-shaped epic of Portuguese 'discovery' (*The Lusiads* 1572); and Roman shaping of slave law in the Dutch-controlled Cape Colony.

Classics served as an imperial proxy and a training ground for civil servants destined for South Africa. Alfred Milner, the High Commissioner after the Anglo-Boer War and the man whose vision most shaped South Africa as an industrial segregated state, studied under the influential classicist Benjamin Jowett at Oxford. Cecil Rhodes, also classically trained, described himself as a 'modern Roman' and dotted his writing with comparisons between the British and Roman empires – although as Hilton points out Rhodes was ever sceptical of an education that was too bookish (Allen forthcoming; Hilton 2007:21). However, the ways in which ideas of classical civilisation were taken up were not simply top-down and were refracted through the fault-lines and contradictions of South African society. The early African elite, mostly graduates from the ivy league Christian mission schools received a literary and classical training and mobilised these resources as they fashioned forms of anti-colonial discourse. As Jonathan Allen (forthcoming) has argued, professional white classicists in the university system, often from Afrikaans backgrounds, and hence 'half in and half out of the imperial system' used classical texts to explore their contradictory attitudes both for and against imperialism.

Both Hilton's and Vasunia's articles speak to this question of civilisation and the classics as contested discursive terrain in colonial India and southern Africa by focusing on the instructive example of Gandhi. Hilton shows that Gandhi's views on civilisation were partly influenced by Edward Carpenter's radical *Civilisation: Its Cause and Cure* (1899), which was grounded in an interesting approach to the ancient Graeco-Roman world and the emerging science of comparative anthropology, especially in relation to India and Africa. The intellectual relationships and affinities he maps out between Gandhi, Carpenter and Olive Schreiner extends our understanding of how, for anti-colonial thinkers like Gandhi who operated in 'cosmopolitan thought zones' (Bose & Manjapra 2010) across continents, South Africa and India framed his thinking and provided the testing ground and opportunities for formulating his distinctive views on the nature of civilisation. Southern Africa and India also provided Gandhi with the opportunity to combine his personal and political struggles with violence with a re-reading of Plato and Socrates. As Phiroze Vasunia argues in his article, Plato and Socrates are not the first names that come to mind in connection with anti-colonialism or spiritual renewal, yet it is by engaging with Socrates in both India and South Africa that Gandhi was able to remould them into insurgent presences, thereby bringing to the fore the transformative potential of such texts as Plato's *Apology* – potential obscured by the way texts such as these were embedded in colonial systems of pedagogy, reference and allusion in both regions.

One of the shared legacies of colonialism in India and southern Africa is of course the English language. As Rajend Mesthrie points out in his article, both regions were affected by the pre-eminence of English as a language of government, administration, education and societal aspirations, yet indigenous languages and their speakers were also resilient in resisting the wholesale shift to English. In this English was unlike Latin as an imperial language, whose spread was generally accompanied by an eradication of local languages. Within the English-speaking world of post-imperial societies, the issues of which language to write in and the colonial associations of English have been and continue to be a source of contention among writers. The differing positions of Chinua Achebe and Ngugi wa Thiong'o on writing in English are an obvious example of this, while RK Narayan's *The English Teacher* (1945) dramatises the difficult linguistic and pedagogical choices English posed to Indians in colonial India. Equally interesting, though, is the way in which English was modified in both regions by non-'native' speakers. There is a vast literature on this, but the South African Indian community is an excellent example, as Mesthrie demonstrates, of a colonially produced diasporic community whose English spans both regions. He explores the links and differences between South African Indian English and Indian English, outlining the factors that gave rise to these connections and contrasts, and rightly stresses that a consideration of English in the postcolonies of India and South Africa has to take into account its multilingual contexts and the convergence between English and major indigenous languages. On the question of this convergence, Francesca Orsini's article outlines how the boundaries between English and Hindi have become increasingly porous in India over the last decade. She shows how both Indian English and 'Hinglish', 'whether with a Hindi or an English matrix', are now publicly recognised and have become symbols of post-liberalisation India in advertising and the media. However, she also stresses the limits of the social and spatial inclusion of 'Hinglish'. In doing so she calls attention to the parallel growth of Hindi as a language of politics and news, and the limited bilingualism and language shift that accompanies English-medium education. 'Hinglish', then, needs to be disaggregated and its complexities unravelled. It is not quite the linguistic and cultural domain envisaged by Thomas Macaulay in the 1830s, when he spoke of colonial rule in India producing 'a class of persons Indian in blood and colour, but English in tastes, in opinions, in morals and in intellect' (Macaulay in Zastoupil & Moir 1999:171) but something far more radicalised and complex, reflecting one of the enduring legacies of empire described by one historian as involving 'the processes of cultural diffusion, export, copying, fusion, mongrelization or interaction' (Howe 2002:126).

Continuing the theme of language, Javed Majeed's article argues that the geographical imagining of India in the Linguistic Survey of India (conducted by the British colonial state from 1894 to 1927) was in conflict with colonial and nationalist mappings of India. It complicated the notion of India as a single and coherent geographical entity, and in doing so it centralised India in a global linguistic geography. Its cartographical exercises were at odds with both the colonial state's investment in a particular geographical image of India and with the later canonical nationalist imagining of India's linguistic geography. The Linguistic Survey's flexibly conceived space of India, he argues, can interleave with a more flexible conception of the term 'African' as argued for by Gwyn Campbell (2010). The Linguistic Survey helps us to open up the term 'Indian' alongside the term 'African' to think both outside and alongside the methodological nationalism that continues to dominate our fields, obscuring the many connections and linkages between our two regions.

The discussion of South African Indian literature has largely followed the trajectories sketched out above, namely a shift from an ethnicised, narrowly diasporic approach to a broader interpretation of this literature as part of South Africa's multiple inheritances as well as part of a bigger transnational canvas in which literary links within the global south have offered themselves as a new template of world literature (Rastogi 2008; Fainman 2010). Neilesh Bose's article situates itself at this cross-roads, examining a play by Ronnie Govender which deals with an event known as the Cato Manor riots (or pogrom as Jon Soske (2009) has recently called it) involving African-Indian violence in a poor area where the two communities had lived in close proximity. Bose discusses how Govender uses the resources of drama and performance as a way to try and explore the complexities and contradictions of this history which have seldom been probed before. He highlights the necessarily flawed and ambiguous forms through which Govender attempts to narrativise these events. In pursuing this analysis, Bose widens the older narrow and ethnicised diasporic frame by imagining Africans and Indians occupying a shared narrative and historiographical space.

Conclusion

South Africa and India have always constituted what we might call a major transnationalism (as opposed to a minor) (Lionnet & Shih 2005). Drawn together by imperial forces, the two regions have been linked by a dense lattice of networks, both real and imaginary, even during the apartheid period. Indeed PK Datta (2007) in his pioneering work on the meanings and reception of the Anglo-Boer War in British India, refers to the two regions as an integrated intellectual space which he terms 'South Africa-India'. This collection locates itself in that space and attempts to extend it by bringing new dimensions to the emerging debate. In so doing, it also seeks to extend our understanding of connective and comparative transnational method and our ways of tracking the pre-histories of the global South.

Notes

1. The event was funded by the King's Annual Fund, the King's India Institute, and the Centre of Indian Studies, University of Witwatersrand.
2. Javed Majeed explores this in his 'Imperial Literary Sensibilities, Self-definitions, and Cosmopolitanism', in P. Bang, C.A. Bayly & W. Scheidel (eds), *The Oxford World History of Empire* (forthcoming).

References

Allen, J. Forthcoming. 'A Competing Discourse on Empire', in G. Parker (ed), *South Africa, Greece and Rome: Classical Confrontations*. Cambridge: Cambridge University Press.

Anderson, C. 2012. *Subaltern Lives. Biographies of Colonialism in the Indian Ocean World, 1790–1920*. Cambridge: Cambridge University Press.

Bayly, C.A. 2011. *Recovering Liberties. Indian Political Thought in the Age of Liberalism and Empire*. Cambridge: Cambridge University Press.

Bose, S. 2006. *A Hundred Horizons. The Indian Ocean in the Age of Global Empire*. Cambridge MA: Harvard University Press.

Bose, S. & Manjapra, K. (eds). 2010. *Cosmopolitan Thought Zones. South Asia and the Global Circulation of Ideas*. New York: Palgrave Macmillan.

Burton, A. 2012. *Brown Over Black: Race and the Politics of Postcolonial Citation*. Gurgaon: Three Essays Collective.

Campbell, G. 2010. 'The Role of Africa in the Emergence of the "Indian Ocean World" Global Economy', in P. Gupta, I. Hofmeyr & M. Pearson (eds), *Eyes Across the Water. Navigating the Indian Ocean*. Pretoria: Unisa Press.

Datta, P.K. 2007. 'The Interlocking Worlds of the Anglo-Boer War in South Africa/India'. *South African Historical Journal* 57:35–59.

Dhupelia-Mesthrie, U. 2007. 'The Place of India in South African History: Academic Scholarship, Past, Present and Future'. *South African Historical Journal* 57:12–34.

Dhupelia-Mesthrie, U. 2012. 'Cultural Crossings from Africa to India: Select Travel Narratives of Indian South Africans from Durban and Cape Town, 1940s to 1990s'. *South African Historical Journal* 64(2):295–312.

Dhupelia-Mesthrie, U. 2014. 'False Fathers and False Sons: Immigration Officials in Cape Town, Documents and Verifying Minor Sons from India in the First Half of the Twentieth Century'. *Kronos* 40(1):99–132.

Erlank, N. 2009. '"God's Family in the World": Transnational and Local Ecumenism's Impact on Inter-church and Inter-racial Dialogue in South Africa in the 1920s and 1930s'. *South African Historical Journal* 61(2):278–97.

Fainman, R. 2010. *Reconsiderations. South African Indian Fiction and the Making of Race in Post-colonial Culture*. Pretoria: Unisa Press.

Gupta, P. 2007. 'Mapping Portuguese Decolonisation in the Indian Ocean: A Research Agenda'. *South African Historical Journal* 57:93–112.

Hilton, J. 2007. 'Introduction', in J. Hilton & A. Gosling (eds), *Alma Parens Originalis?: The Receptions of Classical Literature and Thought in Africa, Europe, the United States, and Cuba*. Bern: Peter Lang.

Hofmeyr, I. 2007. 'The Idea of "Africa" in Indian Nationalism: Reporting the Diaspora in *The Modern Review* 1907–1929'. *South African Historical Review* 57:60–81.

Hofmeyr, I. & Williams, M. 2011. 'South Africa-India: Historical Connections, Cultural Circulations and Socio-political Comparisons', in I. Hofmeyr & M. Williams (eds), *South Africa and India. Shaping the Global South*. Johannesburg: Wits University Press.

Howe, S. 2002. *Empire. A Very Short Introduction*. Oxford: Oxford University Press.

Lionnet, F. & Shih, S.-m. 2005. *Minor Transnationalism*. Durham: Duke University Press.

Macdonald, A. 2012. 'Colonial Trespassers in the Making of South Africa's International Borders, 1900 to c. 1950'. PhD thesis, Cambridge University.

Majeed, J. 1992. *Ungoverned Imaginings. James Mill's The History of British India and Orientalism*. Oxford: Clarendon Press.

Majeed, J. 1999. 'Comparativism and References to Rome in British Imperial Attitudes to India', in C. Edwards (ed), *Roman Presences. Receptions of Rome in European Culture 1789-1945*. Cambridge: Cambridge University Press.

Majeed, J. 2006. 'Gandhi, "Truth" and Translatability'. *Modern Asian Studies* 40(2):303–2.

Majeed, J. 2007. *Muhammad Iqbal: Islam, Aesthetics and Postcolonialism*. London, New York & New Delhi: Routledge.

McKeown, A. 2008. *Melancholy Order: Asian Migration and the Globalization of Borders*. New York: Columbia University Press.

Rastogi, P. 2008. *Afrindian Fictions: Diaspora, Race, and National Desire in South Africa*. Columbus: Ohio State University Press.

Saussy, H. (ed). 2006. *Comparative Literature in an Age of Globalization*. Baltimore: Johns Hopkins University Press.

Soske, J. 2009. '"Wash me Black Again": African Nationalism, the Indian Diaspora, and Kwa-Zulu Natal, 1944–1960'. PhD thesis, University of Toronto.

Spivak, G. 2004. *Death of a Discipline*. New York: Columbia University Press.

Stanziani, A. 2014. *Sailors, Slaves, and Immigrants: Bondage in the Indian Ocean World, 1750–1914*. New York: Palgrave Macmillan.

Vahed, G. 2005. 'Passengers, Partnerships, and Promissory Notes: Gujarati Traders in Colonial Natal, 1870–1920'. *International Journal of African Historical Studies* 38(3):449–79.

Vasunia, P. 2013. *The Classics and Colonial India*. Oxford: Oxford University Press.

Zastoupil, L. & Moir, M. (eds). 1999. *The Great Indian Education Debate: Documents Relating to the Orientalist-Anglicist Controversy of 1781–1843*. London: Curzon.

Gandhi, Carpenter, Schreiner and the Crisis of Modern Civilisation at the Turn of the 20th Century

John Hilton

University of KwaZulu-Natal

In his published works MK Gandhi frequently refers the concept of 'civilisation'. Gandhi divided this concept into two distinct types: modern and ancient. The former he identified chiefly with western industrial and technological civilisation that had, in his view, reduced the West to a state of 'cultural anarchy', while he viewed the latter far more positively. In his Platonic dialogue, Hind Swaraj, *this distinction is drawn very emphatically.* Hind Swaraj *was strongly influenced by Edward Carpenter's essay* Civilisation: Its Cause and Cure, *in which Carpenter draws an analogy between civilisation and disease. Carpenter's essay rested in turn on the earlier anthropological researches of Lewis Morgan in* Ancient Society, *a substantial part of which is devoted to the structure of ancient Greek society, and which largely inspired Friedrich Engels to compose his study of the origin of the family. This article explores the implications of these debates on social structure, attitudes to property, and gender relations, which were shared by Carpenter's close friend Olive Schreiner, the proto-feminist author of* The Story of an African Farm.

In this article I set out to investigate the origins and development of Mohandas Gandhi's thoughts on civilisation. On this subject Gandhi's ideas and behaviour show close affiliation, though realised in very different ways, with those of his contemporary, Edward Carpenter, who in turn had a long-standing correspondence with the South African feminist writer, Olive Schreiner, with whom Gandhi was also independently linked. It is my aim to triangulate these Victorian dissidents and to reveal the extent to which they responded to and made use of ideas from Classical literature and ancient history in formulating their political views about social problems in South Africa and India at the turn of the 20th century. All three of these writers confronted specific underlying problems of civilisation – human sexuality, the place of women in society, and religion – in various ways. From the perspective of South Africa in the 21st century, it is vital that these critics be heard, since they were strikingly prophetic of the future, our present, and it is precisely the appeal to civilisation that has been used so often to justify nationalism, imperialism (especially at the time of the British declaration of war against the South Africa republics in 1899) and later apartheid (see Hilton forthcoming:74–100).[1]

Comparisons between western and Indian civilisation are well known and of long standing, going back ultimately to the traumatic invasion of the Punjab region of India by Alexander III of Macedon in 326 BCE and the subsequent military and diplomatic expeditions into the sub-continent by those who came after him.[2] The shock of this encounter has been likened to the cultural impact of the invasion of meso-America by the Spanish conquistadores, except that it soon became apparent that the cultures of ancient Greece and India showed many more similarities than they did differences (for this see Bosworth 1996). Later histories of India in the 19th century, such as those of James Mill (Mill & Wilson 1858 vol I, book 2, chapter 1:107–22) and William Hunter (1886:163–73) did not fail to include a discussion of these early interactions.[3] However, the invasion of ancient India by the Macedonian Greeks occupies a relatively small part in these later British histories. Far more important in imperial discourse was the comparison between modern, industrialised, western culture and the traditional culture of India. James Mill, in particular, composed a pejorative account of Indian civilisation in his monumental history of the British East India Company,[4] as part of his critique of British imperialism in India, which Mill viewed as a test case in the debate between the utilitarian ideas of Jeremy Bentham and the conservative political principles of Burke (for this, see Majeed 1992:123–50). Mill's one-sided and partisan account of Indian culture was strongly criticised by none other than Horace Hayman Wilson, who later edited his history and completed his account of the East India Company.[5] Wilson believed that a fairer and more positive account would equate Indian civilisation not with the modern West but with the ancient Greeks and Romans.[6] This article shows that Gandhi eschews these earlier discussions of Indian civilisation in favour of the more critical stance of Carpenter and Schreiner, especially at the time of the Second South African War of Independence (1899–1902).

Gandhi on Civilisation

The patronising 19th-century discourse about India found in the writings of Mill and Wilson constitutes the background to Gandhi's remarks on civilisation, which he expressed frequently in his published works.[7] It shows that the differentiation between ancient and modern civilisations had already been firmly established before Gandhi formulated his thoughts on the subject. In addition to making a rigid distinction between the eastern and western type, Gandhi followed Mill and Wilson in sub-dividing the concept of civilisation into modern and ancient modes. The former he identified chiefly with western industrial and technological advances in the late 19th century that had, in his view, reduced the West to a state of 'cultural anarchy' (*CW* 8:374) within the space of what he estimated to be no more than 50 to 100 years.[8] The latter, on the other hand, he generally identified with ancient Indian culture, which he believed had remained unchanged in the subcontinent for thousands of years, although crucially he did envisage the possibility of an entirely new dispensation.[9]

In respect of ancient civilisations in general Gandhi upheld the superiority of the East over the West. For example, in a speech at a political conference at Gujarat on 3 November 1917, he specifically commented on the 'burial of civilisations', including those in the West (*CW* 14:66). He stated: 'We are the children of an ancient nation. We have witnessed the burial of civilisations: those of Rome, Greece and Egypt. Our civilisation abides even as the ocean in spite of its ebbs and flows.'[10] In the same speech, however, he expressed his admiration for the adventurousness, religious spirit, independence, and even the military achievements of the English nation, but argued that it 'has given the place of honour to its commercial instinct. It worships modern civilisation. The ancient ideals have lost their hold on it'. These comments should be seen within the context of the destruction wrought by what he called 'the pandemonium that is going on in Europe' during the First World War, but possibly go back further, to the time of Gandhi's stand-off with Jan Smuts over the issue of the registration of Indians in South Africa (1904–1908),[11] and beyond that to the upheavals in South African society brought about by the Second South African War of Independence (1899–1902) about which both Carpenter and Schreiner wrote critical political pamphlets.

Gandhi's ambivalent attitude to technological progress of the West is well illustrated by his comments on the construction of the Eiffel Tower during the World Exhibition in Paris in 1889. Although this structure set new standards in the construction of tall buildings in steel, Gandhi sympathised with the view of Leo Tolstoy that the building was 'a monument of man's folly, not of his wisdom' (1927:78). Gandhi later came to share Tolstoy's sceptical view of modern civilisation and his advocacy of the radical Christian doctrine of non-violent resistance, as expressed in his treatise *The Kingdom of God is Within You* (1894) and the two men continued to correspond with one another in later years.[12] Grandiose schemes such as the Eiffel Tower had been initiated in Britain too, where in 1892 Sir Edward Watkin started to build a 'New Tower of Babel' to exceed the Eiffel Tower by some 150 feet (Richardson 2013:131–3). However, the plan failed and the building had to be brought down by dynamite, provoking widespread ridicule. Gandhi's most significant concession to modern technology was his use of a printing press, but even here, it has been argued, he slowed down and limited its impact on readers (Hofmeyr 2013).

Gandhi's views on the subject of civilisation changed considerably over time. In 1906, after the Boer War and under the British administration of South Africa, Gandhi organised protests against the segregationist Black Act and the later Asiatic Law Amendment Act on the basis of the universal values of civilisation.[13] On 18 May 1908 Gandhi participated in a debate held at the YMCA in Johannesburg on the question of whether the 'Asiatics and Coloured races were a menace to the Empire' in which he opposed the argument for the separation of the races and rejected the doctrine that 'might is right'. He consistently rejected the tenet of social evolution, on which the colonials (and specifically Cecil Rhodes) relied, that only the fittest survive,[14] and argued for a harmonious blend of eastern and western civilisations:

> I do not mix up or confuse western civilisation with Christian progress ... I think western civilisation also represents tremendous activity, eastern civilisation represents contemplativeness, but it also sometimes represents lethargy. It is necessary that that civilisation should come into contact with that of the west. It is necessary that that civilisation should be quickened with the western spirit ... It is then necessary for these two civilisations to meet and we shall have a different force altogether, by no means a menacing force, by no means a force that disunites, but a force that unites.

Gandhi was not alone in suggesting that the West had something to offer India. Karl Marx, too, suggested in a much earlier article in *The New York Daily Tribune* that precolonial India had been far from a free and egalitarian society.[15] Marx's comments here are to some extent similar in tone to those of Mill in his *History of British India* that was published some five years later. Gandhi's remarks during the YMCA debate, however, clearly need to be interpreted within the context of his objectives in that speech and are not aligned with his views as they are expressed elsewhere.

Later, in India, when campaigning for independence, Gandhi was less accommodating. In his Platonic dialogue, *Hind Swaraj* (1909), Gandhi condemns 'modern civilisation' very emphatically. He writes:

> The British Government in India constitutes a struggle between the Modern Civilisation, which is the Kingdom of Satan, and the Ancient Civilisation, which is the Kingdom of God. The one is the God of War, the other is the God of Love. (Parel 1997:7)

Above all, modern civilisation was anti-Christian.[16] However, Gandhi's hostile attitude in *Hind Swaraj* stemmed in part from the banning of the work in 1910, in part from his distaste for British exploitation of the gold resources of the Transvaal (Parel 1997:41), despite the fact that he had earlier organised an ambulance to serve the cause of the British Empire during the Boer War.[17] As Gandhi explains in his autobiography, his motives for doing this, despite the fact that his 'personal sympathies were all with the Boers' (1927:214) was to empower the Indian community in South Africa by proving their loyalty to the British Empire in a manner consistent with his pacifist beliefs. However, his hopes for raising Indians in South Africa to a position of equality with the British were disappointed and his attitude to British imperialism hardened considerably from this point on, along with the rising tide of criticism of British policy in South Africa expressed by liberal opponents of imperialism, including Schreiner and, through her, Carpenter.

Gandhi was not oblivious to western criticisms of Indian civilisation, especially with regard to what was arguably the most urgent political issue of the day – women's rights. Isabella Fyvie Mayo, a translator of Tolstoy's works and later supporter of Indian rights in the Transvaal, accused Indian men of having no respect for their women and making them work as slaves (*CW* 43:252–5).[18]

It is greatly to his credit that Gandhi, who admired the courage of the English suffragettes greatly (*CW* 6:29–30), took this criticism to heart and continued to advocate the rights of Indian women throughout his life. His support for women's rights began in South Africa, where he successfully supported the controversial immigration of Indian women into the country for the purpose of contracting polygamous marriages with the indentured labourers from India – a practice that had been declared illegal by the Transvaal High Court (*CW* 11:120, 12:215).[19] More generally he clearly saw that the economic disempowerment of Indian women lay at the root of many of the social ills that confronted them: prostitution, female infanticide, child marriage, the purdah, the prohibition against widows remarrying, physical abuse and rape, especially in times of war.[20] It was largely for this reason that he reverted to traditional methods of spinning cloth and burnt saris made with foreign material. In his view, the old-fashioned way of making clothes at least gave women employment and some form of income.[21] Women were crucial to the success of Gandhi's non-violent civil disobedience movement, as he clearly stated in a pungent and pointed epigram:[22] 'For the courage of self-sacrifice woman is any day superior to man as I believe man is to woman for the courage of the brute.'

Finally, while Gandhi was concerned about the destructive consequences of the adoption of modern western civilisation on India, he also referred to its effect on other cultures, especially those he termed 'negroes'. In *Satyagraha in South Africa* (*CW* 29:14–15) he comments in a manner reminiscent of the 'noble savage' ethnographical theme: '"Civilisation"' is gradually making headway among the negroes ... but many, being illiterate and therefore strangers to civilisation, were so far free from many vices, [but] have now become corrupt.' On occasion he noted that Indians could claim a greater affinity with whites than could black Africans 'because of their [the Indians'] illustrious historical past'.[23] On the other hand, he also pointed out the coercive nature of the poll tax imposed on South African blacks. Without it, he contended, they would not have had to labour in the gold and diamond mines. Gandhi's experience of the racial and cultural complexity of South African society, along with his reading of the radical Christian thoughts of Tolstoy, are to a large extent responsible for his trenchant condemnation of the caste system in India and precipitated a glimpse of the possibility of an entirely new future:

> If we look into the future, is it not a heritage we have to leave to posterity, that all the different races commingle and produce a civilization that perhaps the world has not yet seen? There are differences and misunderstandings, but I do believe, in the words of the sacred hymn, 'We shall know each other better when the mists have rolled away'.[24]

Gandhi and Carpenter

Gandhi's attitude towards western civilisation was strongly influenced by Edward Carpenter's essay *Civilisation: Its Cause and Cure* (1921),[25] which is cited in *Hind Swaraj* as written by 'a great English writer' Parel (1997:34). In his short treatise, Carpenter elaborates on Max Nordau's analogy between civilisation and disease, and Gandhi also makes this comparison throughout *Hind* Swaraj (Parel 1997:39–40, 47).[26] Carpenter argued that civilisation would have just as fatal an effect on people living closer to nature in the uncivilised regions of the world as the sicknesses brought to them by the colonisers had already done. He traced the root cause of this condition within western nations to the development of self-consciousness in Man, which Carpenter traces back to the Delphic aphorism 'Know Thyself' (Carpenter 1921:24–5), and the advent of money in Graeco-Roman society. He wrote:

> The growth of wealth, it is shown, and with it the conception of private property, brought on very definite forms of social life; it destroyed the ancient system of society based on the *gens*, that is a society of equals founded upon blood-relationship, and introduced a society of classes founded upon differences of material possession; it destroyed the ancient system of mother-right and inheritance through the female line, and turned the woman into the property of the man. (Carpenter 1921:4–5)

According to Carpenter, the civilisations of England, Rome, Greece, Israel and Egypt, eventually 'succumbed soon after the main symptoms had been developed' (1921:5) to the malaise of civilisation. In the case of Greece, so often the paradigmatic case in such discussions, the Homeric age and the myth of the Golden Age gave way to an aristocratic or timocratic culture as evident in the conservative social thinking of Plato and this in turn degenerated into an anarchic world in which the rabble ruled and society descended into 'caucuses and cackle, competition and universal greed, breaking out in cancerous tyrannies and plutocracies – a mere chaos and confusion of society' (1921:32–3). Carpenter opposed such societies in which there is 'no solidarity such as existed in the ancient tribes and primaeval society, but only disintegration and a dust-heap. The true Democracy has yet to come' (1921:33).

Such ideas clearly rested on the earlier anthropological researches of Lewis Morgan in *Ancient Society* (1964),[27] a work that had also already inspired Engels to compose his study of the origin of the family and the social evolution of Man 'through savagery and barbarism to the beginning of civilisation' (1972:93).[28] In Carpenter's analysis, the Homeric and Spartan Greeks occupied the position of 'advanced barbarism' (Carpenter 1921:6, fn 2, 10),[29] while the Matabele in Africa, for example, who were relatively untouched by civilisation, and had only recently been brought within the British Empire by Leander Jameson and Rhodes, were at the middle stage. Carpenter's essay then proceeds to document the extraordinary physical strength of these African people and their great social cohesion. Carpenter goes on to note a 'loss of unity' in societies that progress to a higher plane and traces the similarities between this process and scientific accounts of disease within living organisms and within the cosmos. In this he anticipates the idea of 'holism' advocated by his South African contemporary, Jan Smuts, and later advocated by Schreiner (Smuts 1926). The cure for this dissociation, is his view, was for Man to reintegrate himself within nature and to recognise the communal nature of society, in the process recovering the same harmonious relationship between himself and the natural world as that displayed by the Greeks in creating architecture such as the Parthenon. It is typical of Carpenter that he balances this Classical reference with one drawn from comparative anthropology; the Bushmen of South Africa, he notes, live close to nature and 'can hide themselves and become indistinguishable on a slope of bare rock' (Carpenter 1921:39). The recent work by Edward Tylor and James Frazer had given body to the study of human evolution and had recently been ably exploited by the Scottish Classicist Andrew Lang.[30] Should this reintegration of Man with nature happen, Carpenter foresaw the return of nature-religions such as those prevalent in the ancient world. Given that the world had shrunk with the advent of improved means of transport and communications, a 'complex human communism' would evolve together with 'individual freedom and savagery' that would balance and correct each other.

Carpenter's understanding of the differences between eastern and western civilisation and the place of sex in religion was broadened by a trip he took to India at the invitation of his Sri Lankan nationalist friend Ponnambalam Arunáchalam, whom he had met at Cambridge and who had first brought both Indian religious thought and the oppression of India under the Raj to his attention.[31] What impressed Carpenter most on his visit was the sexual openness of the Ceylonese towards homosexuality that was similar, in his view, to the attitude of the Classical Greeks. Carpenter who belonged to what he called the 'intermediate' sexual type, found this freedom liberating in contrast with the repressive attitude of Victorian society on the question. Carpenter frequently wrote on the place of 'homogenic love' in society, comparing it with other cultures and especially with the antecedents in Greek literature. In his view – one that anticipated Freud's in *Civilisation and its Discontents* (1920) – men and women in the Christianised West needed to recognise that they were sexually repressed and to return to a more natural pagan way of life. He had already prophesied a return to nature religions in *Civilisation*, but took this analysis further in *Pagan and Christian Creeds: Their Origin and Meaning* (1920). In this work he describes a night festival of Taipusam that he had earlier witnessed on his trip to Sri Lanka (Carpenter 1920:264–6; compare also Carpenter 1910:116–36). He suggests that this 'fragment of ancient ritual' as he termed it, could be used in a future World Religion that would reflect the third stage of human consciousness (after the primitive prelapsarian stage, and the development of human self-consciousness after the Fall).

Carpenter argued that homosexuality in Greek society had initially not been accompanied by a decline in the status of women. This he made clear in his analysis of the position of women in Greek society in the newly established feminist journal *The New Freewoman* in August 1913, repeated in *Intermediate Types* (Carpenter 1914:104–16). Indeed, following the thesis of Engels that the economic empowerment of men in the Classical period of Greece had been accompanied by the 'world-historic defeat' of the female sex, Carpenter actively supported the political rights of women, as he demonstrated in *Woman and her*

Place in Society (1894), despite the patronising tone he adopts from time to time in this pamphlet. As he stated there (1894:24): 'the liberation of Woman from her position of dependence on Man is the very next step in her line of progress, and that her status is not likely to improve until she is able face Man on an equality.' The final paragraph of *Woman and her Place in Society* (1894:41) invokes the presence of ancient Greek goddesses to witness the emergence of a grander type of future Woman 'fearless and untamed', who would combine 'a broad sense with sensibility, the passion for Man with the love of Man' and set aside the conventions that limited her.

Carpenter's ideas were synthesised in his book, *The Art of Creation: Essays on the Self and Its Powers* (1904). This remarkable study brings together the *Upanishads*, Plato, Jesus of Nazareth and Paul of Tarsus, Plotinus, and European philosophy of the 17th, 18th and 19th centuries. Carpenter begins with the origin of consciousness in biological evolution, but he credits the influence of eastern ideas in making the mind and the emotions more important than matter in the process of creation (1904:10–11). Consciousness, in his psychological scheme, is threefold: first there is simple consciousness in which subject and object are undifferentiated, next the consciousness of Self becomes more pronounced, and in the final stage of Cosmic Consciousness, the individual perceives, through some form of mystical intuition, that subject and object are one.[32] Carpenter looks to the *Upanishads* for evidence of his third stage of consciousness (1904:57–8) and to Plato for an account of psychological development from emotions to metaphysical Ideas, such as Justice, Goodness and Beauty (1904:106–22).[33] Carpenter adds a unique consideration of heredity to his analysis of Plato, explaining different cultural and racial expressions of innate and essential Ideas to the effect of different evolutionary environments in which they are manifested. Thus the gods of different races differ but all are manifestations of a deeper 'World Self' (1904:126) apprehended through a process of recollection (*anamnēsis*, as explained in the *Phaedrus*, 1904:130). Christian ideals developed under the Roman Empire in much the same way, according to Carpenter, that believers in India apprehended the Buddha (1904:152–3). Here Carpenter anticipates Richard Dawkins' theory of 'memes' (1989), adducing the visions of gods by mystics in India in support of his analysis.

Carpenter, Schreiner, and Gandhi

Over the years, Carpenter had carried on a sustained friendship with the early feminist author Olive Schreiner, whose *Story of an African Farm* (1883) had attracted his attention (as well as that of Havelock Ellis) for her views on sexuality and the position of women in society and who had alerted him to the threat of war in South Africa.[34] Schreiner was the daughter of a Lutheran father, Gottlob, and a Wesleyan English mother, Rebecca Lyndall, both members of Dr John Philip's London Missionary Society, who had been sent to the South African frontier in the early 19th century on a 'civilizing mission' (Philip 1828; First & Scott 1980:30–1). Raised speaking English only, beaten severely as a child by her mother for speaking Afrikaans, and belonging to a family that rapidly rose to occupy senior positions in British imperial politics at the Cape, Schreiner was an articulate rebel against the imperial British line and supported the Boer cause strongly. In 1899 she wrote a political pamphlet, *An English South African's View of the Situation*, in which she opposed the British declaration of war, warning that it would result in desperate resistance from the Boers who would lay down their lives in the same way that the 300 Spartans had at Thermopylae, or, as she explains in a far more vivid simile, as she had seen a *meerkat* would do, when taken into the mouth of a dog (Schreiner 1899:82, 90). In a typically emotional passage at the conclusion of this piece, in which she placed herself in the position of the Roman soldier Gaius Mucius Scaevola, as told by Livy (2.12). Schreiner wrote: '. . . rather than strike down one South African man fighting for freedom we would take this right hand and hold it in the fire until nothing was left of it but a charred and blackened bone' (1899:90). She and her husband campaigned for the Boer cause in the United Kingdom under the banner of the South African Conciliation Committee, on which Gilbert Murray, the Regius Professor of Greek at Oxford, served.

Carpenter's own anti-war pamphlet, *Boer and Briton*, followed soon after Schreiner's publication in 1900. In it, Carpenter argued that the opposing forces were very unequal; using Aesop's fable of the Wolf and the Lamb he suggested that just as it was absurd to imagine the lamb devouring the wolf so it was ridiculous to think that the Transvaal Republic would be able to defeat the British Empire. In Carpenter's view the war was driven by capitalist greed and Jingo-Imperialism to the detriment of the finer qualities that the British Empire had to offer, such as 'our marvellous command of materials, our resource, tradition, our splendid organising capacity'. If these qualities were allowed to flourish then Britons would be able to win over the subject peoples of the Empire, 'to heal race-divisions, to build an empire in their hearts, the greatest the world has ever seen!' (1900:4). Carpenter's position on the war was far more remote and ideological than Schreiner's impassioned rhetoric.

Despite her relatively impoverished background, Schreiner was a highly educated woman with a good grasp of the Classics and modern political theory and the crisis in western civilisation. At the age of 16 she read Herbert Spencer's *First Principles* (1862) – a work that she claimed inspired her belief in the underlying animism of nature in a way 'akin to when Christianity burst on the Roman world'.[35] In a letter to her friend, Alfred Mattison, she also wrote, under conditions of martial law imposed by the British in Beaufort West in 1901, of her increasing respect for Edward Gibbon's *History of the Decline and Fall of the Roman Empire*, which she read a number of times in her life. She imagined that the early Christians had invented the idea of Hell because they saw it in action, as she did, every day, during the British occupation of the town. Gibbon's *Decline and Fall* clearly had more than a conventional significance for her. On 21 January 1889 she had written to Carpenter criticising him for comments he had made, probably in *Civilisation: Its Cause and Cure*, about the intellect, which

Schreiner deemed to be as important as nature as a source of inspiration ('the same joy and peace comes to my little soul reading . . . Gibbon's Decline and Fall that comes to it from looking at a sunset behind these tall mountains'). Schreiner's assessment of 'modern civilisation' was more balanced than Carpenter's[36] and also more original. Previously already, in 1887, she had written to Havelock Ellis, claiming that the idea that the decline of Rome had come about because of 'conditions of women' such as herself was her own original thought.[37] On 4 July 1911 she wrote again, in her characteristically loose grammatical and orthographical style, to Carpenter,[38] correcting his suggestion that her reading of *Decline and Fall* had influenced her views on the position of women in society as expressed in *Woman and Labour* (1911):

> Its a curious idea of yours that Gibbon! of all people had anything to do with my view in the book. Its always seemed strange to me that Gibbon seems almost to ignore the existence of woman! & certainly never touches on any problem of sex. Where he is valuable is in his dissection of the rise of Christianity but above all he, & he only, paints widely & clearly the causes which have led to the division of Europe into its present form of nations. Monson's Rome,[39] now, teams with interesting information with regard to woman; & all the old Greek plays & Homer, & even dear old Heroditus pours light on the question of woman & her position in ancient times.

In 1912 thoughts of the decadence of western civilisation were still in her mind. Now, however, she retrospectively applied the idea to England's loss of honour as a result of the Boer War. Schreiner felt that the decline in the ancient world from Homer, Euripides, Plato and Aristotle to Tacitus was mirrored in the fall-off of England from the time of Jane Austen to the first decade of the new 20th century.[40]

Schreiner was nevertheless inspired in her campaign by Hellenistic idealism. In her later years, she expressed her special admiration for Euripides, whose plays she read in Gilbert Murray's translations,[41] and even claimed to prefer him to Shakespeare.[42] She wrote in 1910 – three years before Murray first wrote *Euripides and his Age*:[43] 'It is his outlook on life, that fierce, restrained questioning of the mystery of existence, and also his deep understanding of woman's position that touches one so', and in 1911:

> I wish I knew Greek perfectly. I've been having the most blissful joy reading Gilbert Murray's translations of Euripides plays. They are glorious. For the last 20 years all the books that have given me the most pleasure are the translations of Greek & Latin writers. Jowel's Plato[44] & all the prose writers one has been able to get at, but Gilbert Murray is the only man who has made Greek poetry live in English. I like Euripides more even if be possible than our sweet Will Shakespeare he seems closer to me – but it's ill judging between the dear Gods – they each sit on their own throne with a crown of eternal glory on their heads.[45]

In a letter to Mrs Rhys Davids[46] she comments specifically about how Euripides had handled the role of Helen in *Trojan Women*:

> The reading of Gilbert Murray's translations of Euripides lately has been a revelation of joy to me. The wonderful thing to me is that any man could have written of women as he does. But genius has no limit of sex or race. It's curious to sit here in this little

> house in the karroo veld and feel that perhaps the thing nearest to you in the world is the brain of that old Greek dead now these two thousand years. We who can't read Greek should be so grateful to Gilbert Murray for giving him to us. I'm so glad I didn't die before I had him.

Schreiner did not only take up the cause of women, however. Although she tended to view the races in South Africa in evolutionary terms (Krebs 1997:427–4), her political activism extended also to the position of Indians, Blacks and Jews in South Africa. Her last thoughts before death, expressed in her short essay *The Dawn of Civilisation* (1923b), testify to her hope that cruelty and oppression in all forms would eventually come to an end. She corresponded regularly with Hermann Kallenbach, the wealthy Jewish architect who donated Tolstoy Farm in the Transvaal to Gandhi and his group.[47] Gandhi wrote to Carpenter on 29 July 1911 asking him to meet Kallenbach. Since Schreiner was a close acquaintance of Carpenter's it is probable that it was she who facilitated the connection. At any rate, Schreiner campaigned against racial and sexual oppression in South Africa and equated the two forms of injustice ('a man & a woman stand in the same relation to each other as a white-man & a black-man') (quoted by Tsuzuki 1980:131). When Carpenter visited India, Schreiner supported his interest in the subcontinent,[48] and at the time of the formation of the Union of South Africa, she took up the cause of South African Indians herself.[49] On 23 April 1912 Schreiner suggested to her friend, Betty Molteno, that she should visit Gandhi at Tolstoy Farm. That Molteno did so is apparent from a letter from Gandhi to Alice Greene, in which the visit is mentioned.[50] When war broke out in Europe in 1914, Gandhi invited Schreiner to a meeting the purpose of which was to discuss how India should respond. She rejected the invitation on the grounds that she was completely opposed to war in general but allied herself as an outsider to Europe in solidarity with Gandhi.[51]

Conclusions

This article has endeavoured to contextualise Gandhi's thoughts on civilisation by showing that the earlier 19th-century discourse comparing the West and India, to the detriment of the latter, was later replaced by a less confident and more critical paradigm evident in the writings of critics of western society such as Carpenter and Schreiner. The more reflective and nuanced views of all three thinkers, but especially the latter two, were informed by a deeper understanding of the place of modern societies in the overall development of humanity since the formative Greco-Roman period. By putting the social problems of their time into a wider perspective, both chronologically and culturally, they were able to formulate a more universal conception of the place in society of individuals dislodged by the fragmenting forces of modern technologies of travel, colonialism, and communication. All three had momentary insights into a better world free from hostility and conflict – Gandhi foreseeing greater racial integration, especially in South Africa, Carpenter envisaging a more evolved Cosmic Consciousness, and Schreiner looking forward to an era of universal peace.

Throughout his writings, Gandhi insisted that he did not aspire to articulate new ideas. Instead he applied a combination of progressive feminist ideas and traditional spiritual solutions – embracing both the Christian model of resistance to the imperial might of Rome as expressed in Christ's Sermon on the Mount and the Indian concept of non-violence (*ahimsa*) – to the problems of the day. Above all, he rejected the adoption of the materialism of modern western civilisation as the road for Indian development. His reading of Carpenter reinforced this conviction. Carpenter's essay was grounded in a complex nexus of ideas including an awareness, reinforced by analogies with the ancient Greco-Roman world and the emerging science of comparative anthropology, especially in relation to Africa and India, of how the revolution in science and technology, the expansion of the British Empire, and the advent of ideas of social evolution in the second half of the 19th century was driving British society into an aggressive / oppressive / repressive phase of materialism that led to the catastrophic wars in South Africa and Europe in the first years of the 20th century. Carpenter's long-standing friendship and correspondence with Schreiner and others alerted him to the social problems of what would now be termed the developing world and pointed him and his readers, including Gandhi, towards what they saw as a possible solution – the reintegration of western civilisation into the underlying harmony of nature and thereby the strengthening of a non-violent pacifist movement against imperialism and warfare.

Acknowledgements

I acknowledge the financial support of the National Research Foundation of South Africa and research funding of the Department of Higher Education and Training of South Africa. I am grateful to King's College, London, for the invitation to attend the India and South Africa Conference: Comparisons, Confluences and Contrasts, 5–6 October 2012 and for its generous hospitality during this time.

Notes

1. For the use of the term 'civilisation' at the height of the modern period, see the published radio broadcasts of KD White (1957), discussed by Edmund Richardson (2013:161–9, especially) reviewed by Christopher Stray (2014) and Hilton (2014). It is easy to misjudge the discourse about civilisation in South Africa. Errol Harris (1952), for example, despite its unpromising title, is a liberal pamphlet, published by the Institute of Race Relations, which argues that white civilisation would best be preserved by racial integration rather than apartheid.

2. The bibliography on this is extensive. For general histories of the invasions, see Thapar (1990); Tarn (1951); Narain (1957). For a comparison between the two cultures, see Sedlar (1980), Bannerjee (1981).
3. See also the earlier account of Mathurin Veyssière de la Croze's *History of Christianity in the Indies* (1724), which argued that linga worship was essentially the worship of Osiris and Bacchus (as noted by Majeed 1992:14). Colonialist histories of India are discussed by Ranajit Guha (1998:2–3, especially): 'Indian history, assimilated thereby [i.e. by coloniast histories] to the history of Great Britain, would henceforth be used as a comprehensive measure of difference between the peoples of these two countries. Politically that difference was spelled out as one between rulers and the ruled; ethnically, between a white Herrenvolk and blacks; materially, between a prosperous Western power and its poor Asian subjects; culturally, between high and lower levels of civilisation, between the superior religion of Christianity and indigenous belief system made up of superstitition and barbarism – all adding up to an irreconcilable difference between colonizer and colonized.'
4. Especially vol 2, book 2, chapter 10:107–64: 'General Reflections: The importance of the inquiry into the state of civilisation among the Hindus.' Mill held that Indian accounts of their past were largely fictional, that they had enjoyed no enlightened monarchical governments but rather had been subjected to cruel despotisms, that they had not constructed usable roads, that their wealth was grossly exaggerated, that their armies were ill-disciplined and incompetent, that they had no coherent legal code, that they mistreated women and animals, that they resembled the ancient Egyptians in being unclean, indecent and debauched, and so on.
5. Volumes 7–9, 1805–1835. See especially Wilson's preface to his edition of Mill's history (Mill & Wilson 1858, vols 7–9:xii). Wilson believed that Mill's negative account of Indian culture negatively influenced the attitudes of imperial administrators who usually read his work before setting out to India (Mill & Wilson 1858, vols 7–9:xii).
6. See the note at vol 2, book 2, chapter 10:164: 'The Hindus, by the character of their institutions, and by the depressing influence of foreign subjugation, are apparently what they were at least three centuries before the Christian era. Two thousand years have done nothing for them, everything for us. We must, therefore, in fairness, compare them with their contemporaries, with the people of antiquity; and we shall then have reason to believe, that they occupied a very foremost station amongst the nations . . . Whatever defects may be justly imputed to their religion, their government, their laws, their literature, their sciences, their arts, as contrasted with the same proofs of civilisation in modern Europe, it will not be disputed by any impartial and candid critic, that as far as we have the means of instituting a comparison, the Hindus were in all these respects quite as civilized as the most civilized nation of the ancient world, and in as early times as any of which records or traditions remain.' For later systematic comparisons between the Roman and Indian Empires, see Bryce (1914); Hilton (forthcoming). For the role of the Classics in shaping ideas and practices of the British administration of India, see Vasunia (2013).
7. For Gandhi's thoughts on civilisation see Iyer (1973:23–36). Gandhi (1869–1948) clearly knew the work of Hunter (*Collected Works* [hereafter *CW*] 1:182, 288–9, 29:22 and Gandhi 1927:404) and read widely while in prison (Frederic William Farrar's *Seekers after God*, for example, *CW* 25:82–7).
8. Many writers on Gandhi have commented on his rejection of all aspects of modern western civilisation, even when he relied on them as he did on the railways and telegraph (Lelyveld 2011:91–2). Compare also Sethia & Narayan (2013); Swan (1985:177); Erikson (1970:217–26).
9. Speech on Indian Civilisation, Indore (30 March 1918), *CW* 14:298–300. See *CW* <http://www.gandhiserve.org/e/cwmg/cwmg.htm> (accessed 30 June 2014), but the references in this article are to the print edition consulted at the documentation centre of the University of KwaZulu-Natal, Westville. The reference to this speech in the online version is vol 16:376–8.

10. Ironically, Richard Sorabji (2012) has recently amply demonstrated how similar Gandhi's philosophy was to the thinking of the ancient Stoics. Compare also Mehdi (2007). Sorabji states firmly (2012:1) that there is no question of any 'influence' of Stoic ideas on Gandhi, or vice versa, however.
11. *CW* 13:260–4, speech at the Gurukil Anniversary (20 March 1916). Gandhi's antipathy to modern western civilisation have been traced to his traumatic experience of the new technology of fingerprinting in South Africa (1904–1908). For this, see Breckenridge (2011:331–48).
12. See Gandhi's comments in his autobiography (1927:138): 'Tolstoy's *The Kingdom of God is Within You*' overwhelmed me.' Gandhi later named his communal farm in the Transvaal after Tolstoy.
13. On segregationist legislation introduced under the British administration of South Africa prior to the Union in 1910, see Du Toit (2005:419-48, especially 432 ff).
14. *CW* 8:244–5 taken from *Indian Opinion* 13 June 1908. For Gandhi's rejection of the doctrine of the 'survival of the fittest' see also *CW* 50:310. For Rhodes and social evolution, see Hilton (forthcoming).
15. 'The British Rule in India', Karl Marx, *The New York Daily Tribune* 25 June 1853. Marx was criticised for these remarks by Saïd (1978:153–7). For a full discussion exploring some of the complexities of these statements, see Ahmad (1992:221–42).
16. *CW* 13:44, letter to Esther Fearing Bettiah (9 June 1917).
17. For the Boer War as a life-changing experience for Gandhi, see Vahed (2000:201–19). On the ambulance service, see Lelyveld (2011:44–8).
18. See also the comments of Mill (1878 vol 1, book 2, chapter 7:309–19).
19. Compare also *Rand Daily Mail* 29 September 1913; Naidu (1921:35–8).
20. For these issues see Joshi (1988).
21. On the burning of saris made of foreign cloth, see *CW* 20:495 (*Young India* 11 August 1921).
22. *CW* 68:52–3 on 'Woman's special mission'.
23. The quotation is taken from Bhana & Vahed (2005:14): 'Fully aware that White rulers intended to exclude indigenous peoples from the system, Gandhi argued that "Indians" could indeed claim great affinity to Western civilisation because of their illustrious historical past. By contrast, the indigenous populations, referred to variously as "natives" and "kaffirs", displayed no such advanced levels of development.' For extenuating comments, see Lelyveld (2011:58–9).
24. Excerpt from 1908 YMCA debate on the role of Asiatics in the Empire, see note 14 above. The passage quoted in the text is also highlighted and well contextualised by Lelyveld (2011:60).
25. On Carpenter, see Rowbotham (2008). It is well known that Carpenter owed much to Tolstoy, John Ruskin's Christian-socialist critique of the Victorian political economy in *Unto this Last* (1860), and Max Nordau's Zionist treatise *Degeneration* (1892).
26. However, note Parel (1997:38): 'Civilisation is not an incurable disease, but it should never be forgotten that the English people are at present afflicted by it.'
27. Morgan gave Carpenter the title of his poetic anthology, *Towards Democracy*, since he believed modern western civilisation needed to move on to a fuller democracy (Morgan 1964:552).
28. For the discussion of the transition of society from barbarism to civilisation, see Engels (1972:217–37); White (1964). For other Marxist analyses of Ancient History see Wood (1981:3–22; see also the UCT Classicist Benjamin Farrington (1938), whom Schreiner met in Cape Town in September 1920 (Olive Schreiner BC16/Box7/Fold4/Mar-Dec1920/20 in the MS archive of the University of Cape Town). On Farrington's Marxist views, see Atkinson (2010:671–92, forthcoming:356–79). The influence of Darwinian evolution is evident in much of this discussion. Desmond & Moore (2010) have recently traced the inspiration for Darwin's scientific endeavours to the debate over slavery in British society.
29. Carpenter adduces the myth of the Golden Age as evidence of the Greek awareness of a social and cultural decline (1921:10). Carpenter had chosen Mathematics over Classics at Cambridge,

which his brother Charles felt was a mistake (see the correspondence between the two brothers in MSS 349/66-69 in the Sheffield archive, cited by Copley (2006:38–9). Nevertheless, Edward frequently refers to the Classics in his writings and had clearly read extensively in the field.

30. For Lang, see Hilton (2011:107–28). See Lang (1887) for an example of his anthropologically-inspired work.
31. For the influence of Indian thought on Carpenter, see Barua (1991:127–50). For the relationship between his homosexuality and 'Orientalism' see Bakshi (1990:151–77); Copley (2006:1–104). Arunachalam gave Carpenter a copy of the *Bhagavad Gita*, according to Copley (2006:22).
32. Although Carpenter makes no reference to his contemporary, Sigmund Freud, their views on this three-stage psychological development are remarkably congruent. Both accounts were strongly influenced by Plato. For Freud and Plato, see Santas (1988).
33. Like Gandhi, Carpenter found inspiration in the writings of Tolstoy, especially his essay 'What is Art?' (1930:182–3). This essay was translated by Aylmer Maude in 1904, the same year in which Carpenter's book *The Art of Creation* was published.
34. Carpenter (1927:134) calls Schreiner 'that great and original authoress' whose 'mental penetration and vigour' he had the 'greatest respect' for. Carpenter's discussion of the hostility between the sexes as reflected in sculptures of the Amazons and in Aristophanes' *Lysistrata* reflects that of Schreiner (1923a:194–7).
35. For the underlying 'animist' beliefs of Schreiner, which she held in common with Edward Carpenter, see Knechtel (2010:259–82). The quotation is from a letter by Havelock Ellis (28 March 1884).
36. See Schreiner (1923a:322): 'Whatever is evil in modern civilisation is ours, and also whatever is good.'
37. Letter 259, to Havelock Ellis (12 December 1887).
38. Olive Schreiner: Edward Carpenter SMD 30/32/j (National Literary Museum, Grahamstown). The letters of Olive Schreiner are available online <http://www.oliveschreiner.org>.
39. Theodor Mommsen, the famous German historian and Nobel laureate (1902), must be meant. See Rebenich (2002); Wiesehöfer (2005).
40. Olive Schreiner to Havelock Ellis (25 August 1912) in the Harry Ransom Centre at the University of Texas at Austin: HRC/UNCAT/OS-148-a.
41. Letter 492, to Mrs Francis Smith (20 November 1910).
42. Letter 488, to Anna Purcell (sometime in 1910).
43. Letter 492 (September 1913). On Murray, see West (1984); Wilson (1987); Stray (2007).
44. Benjamin Jowett, the Master of Balliol College, Oxford, and well-known translator of the works of Plato is of course meant, see Faber (1957).
45. Letter 359/97, to Edward Carpenter in the Sheffield archives (28 April 1911). Compare also her feminist reading of Gilbert Murray's translation of Euripides' *Iphigeneia* (which one is not mentioned) in a letter to Frederick Pethick-Lawrence (August 1910): Olive Schreiner BC16/Box8/Fold4/MMPr/AssortedCorres/FredPL/15.
46. Letter 484, written from De Aar (13 April 1913).
47. On Gandhi's relationship with Kallenbach, see Lelyveld (2011:88–97).
48. Letter 359/51 in the Sheffield archive (22 April 1891).
49. Letter 484, to Caroline Rhys Davids (12 April 1910).
50. Both letters are in the UCT MS archive at Olive Schreiner BC16/Box5/Fold1/1912/15.
51. Letter to Herman Kallenbach in the National Library of South Africa in Cape Town Msc26/23.4 (2 October 1914).

References

Ahmad, A. 1992. *In Theory: Classes, Nations, Literatures*. London: Verso.

Atkinson, J. 2010. 'Benjamin Farrington: Cape Town and the Shaping of a Public Intellectual'. *South African Historical Journal* 28:671–92.

Atkinson, J. Forthcoming. 'Benjamin Farrington and the Science of Swerve', in Parker (ed), *South Africa, Greece and Rome: Classical Confrontations*, 356–379. Cambridge University Press.
Bakshi, P.K. 1990. 'Homosexuality and Orientalism: Edward Carpenter's Journey to the East', in T. Brown (ed), *Edward Carpenter and Late Victorian Radicalism*. London: Frank Cass.
Bannerjee, G.N. 1981. *Hellenism in Ancient India*. New Delhi: Munshiram Manoharlal.
Barua, D.K. 1991. *Edward Carpenter 1844–1929: An Apostle of Freedom*. Burdwan: University of Burdwan.
Bhana, S. & Vahed, G. 2005. *The Making of a Political Reformer; Gandhi in South Africa, 1893–1914*. New Delhi: Manohar.
Bosworth, A.B. 1996. *Alexander and the East: The Tragedy of Triumph*. Oxford: Oxford University Press.
Breckenridge, K. 2011. 'Gandhi's Progressive Disillusionment: Thumbs, Fingers, and the Rejection of Scientific Modernism'. *Hind Swaraj. Public Culture* 23(2):331–48.
Bryce, J. 1914. *The Ancient Roman Empire and the British Empire in India: The Diffusion of Roman and English Law Throughout the World; Two Historical Studies*. London & New York: Oxford University Press.
Carpenter, E. 1894. *Woman, and her Place in a Free Society*. Manchester: Labour Press Society.
Carpenter, E. 1900. *Boer and Briton*. Manchester: Labour Press.
Carpenter, E. 1904. *The Art of Creation: Essays on the Self and its Powers*. London: George Allen & Unwin.
Carpenter, E. 1910. *From Adam's Peak to Elephanta: Sketches in Ceylon and India*. London: Swan, Sonnenschein & Co.
Carpenter, E. 1914. *Intermediate Types Among Primitive Folk: A Study in Social Evolution*. London: George Allen & Unwin.
Carpenter, E. 1920. *Pagan and Christian Creeds: Their Origin and Meaning*. London: George Allen & Unwin.
Carpenter, E. 1921 (first printed 1899). *Civilisation: Its Cause and Cure, and Other Essays*. London: George Allen & Unwin.
Carpenter, E. 1927. *Light from the East Being Letters on Gnanam, The Divine Knowledge*. London: George Allen & Unwin.
Copley, A.R.H. 2006. *A Spiritual Bloomsbury: Hinduism and Homosexuality in the Lives and Writings of Edward Carpenter, E.M. Forster, and Christopher Isherwood*. Lanham, MD & Oxford: Lexington Books.
Dawkins, R. 1989 (first published 1976). *The Selfish Gene*. Oxford: Oxford University Press.
Desmond, A. & Moore, J. 2010. *Darwin's Sacred Cause: Race, Slavery and the Quest for Human Origins*. London: Penguin.
Du Toit, A. 2005. 'Experiments with Truth and Justice in South Africa'. *Journal of South African Studies* 31(2):419–48.
Engels, F. 1972 (translated by E.B. Leacock; first published 1884). *The Origin of the Family, Private Property and the State in the Light of the Researches of Lewis H. Morgan*. London: Lawrence & Wishart.
Erikson, E. 1970. *Gandhi's Truth: On the Origins of Militant Non-violence*. London: Faber and Faber Ltd.
Faber, G. 1957. *Jowett: A Portrait with a Background*. London: Faber and Faber Ltd.
Farrington, B. 1938. *The Civilisation of Greece and Rome*. London: Victor Gollancz.
First, R. & Scott, A. 1980. *Olive Schreiner: A Biography*. London: The Women's Press.
Gandhi, M. K. 1869–1948. *The Collected Works of Mahatma Gandhi* [*CW*] 100 volumes. Delhi: Publications Division: Ministry of Information and Broadcasting, India.
Gandhi, M.K. 1927. *An Autobiography or the Story of my Experiments with Truth*. Ahmedabad: Navajivan Trust.
Guha, R. 1998. *Dominance Without Hegemony: History and Power in Colonial India*. Cambridge, MA & London: Oxford University Press.
Harris, E.E. 1952. *'White' Civilisation: How it is Threatened and How it can be Preserved in South Africa*. Johannesburg: South African Institute of Race Relations.
Hilton, J.L. 2011. 'Andrew Lang, Comparative Anthropology and the Classics in the African Romances of Rider Haggard'. *Akroterion* 56:107–28.

Hilton, J.L. 2014. 'Review of E Richardson *Classical Victorians: Scholars, Scoundrels and Generals in Pursuit of Antiquity. Classics after Antiquity*'. *Acta Classica* 57 <http://www.casa-kvsa.org.za/AC57-Hilton.pdf>.

Hilton, J.L. Forthcoming. 'Cecil Rhodes, the Classics and Imperialism', in Parker (ed), *South Africa, Greece And Rome: Classical Confrontations*, 74–100. Cambridge University Press. <http://dx.doi.org/10.15731/AClass.057.19>.

Hofmeyr, I. 2013. *Gandhi's Printing Press: Experiments in Slow Reading*. Cambridge, MA & London: Harvard University Press.

Hunter, W.W. 1886. *The Indian Empire: Its People, History and Products*. London: Trubner & Co Ltd.

Iyer, R.N. 1973. *The Moral and Political Thought of Mahatma Gandhi*. Oxford: Oxford University Press.

Joshi, P. 1988. *Gandhi on Women*. Ahmedabad: Navajihan Trust.

Knechtel, R. 2010. 'Olive Schreiner's Pagan Animism: An Underlying Unity'. *English Literature in Transition* 53(3):259–82.

Krebs, P.M. 1997. 'Olive Schreiner's Racialization of South Africa'. *Victorian Studies* 40(3):427–44.

Lang, A. 1887. *Myth, Ritual and Religion*. 2 volumes. London: Longman.

Lelyveld, J. 2011. *Great Soul: Mahatma Gandhi and His Struggle with India*. New York: Knopf.

Majeed, J. 1992. *Ungoverned Imaginings James Mill's* The History of British India *and Orientalism*. Oxford: Clarendon Press.

Mehdi, S.M. 2007. 'The Political Dimension of The Contemplative Life: Engagement and Disengagement in Plato, Seneca and Gandhi'. PhD Philosophy, McGill University, Montreal.

Mill, J. & Wilson, H.H. 1858. *The History of British India*. 9 volumes. London: James Madden.

Morgan, L.H. 1964 (first published 1877). *Ancient Society*. Cambridge, MA: The Belknap Press.

Murray, G. 1913. *Euripides and His Age*. London: Thornton Butterworth.

Naidu, S. 1921. *M.K. Gandhi: Life, Writings and Speeches*. Madras: Ganesh & Co.

Narain, A.K. 1957. *The Indo-Greeks*. Delhi & Oxford: Oxford University Press.

Parel, A.J. (ed). 1997. *M.K. Gandhi: Hind Swaraj and Other Papers*. Cambridge: Cambridge University Press.

Parker, G. (ed). 2015. *South Africa, Greece and Rome: Classical Confrontations*. Cambridge: Cambridge University Press.

Philip, J. 1828. *Researches in South Africa*. 2 volumes. London: James Duncan.

Rebenich, S. 2002. *Theodor Mommsen: Eine Biographie*. München: C.H. Beck Verlag.

Richardson, E. 2013. *Classical Victorians: Scholars, Scoundrels and Generals in Pursuit of Antiquity*. Cambridge: Cambridge University Press.

Rowbotham, S. 2008. *Edward Carpenter: A Life of Liberty and Love*. London & New York: Verso.

Saïd, E.W. 1978. *Orientalism: Western Conceptions of the Orient*. London & New York: Penguin.

Santas, G. 1988. *Plato and Freud: Two Theories of Love*. Oxford: Oxford University Press.

Schreiner, O. 1899. *An English South African's View of the Situation: Words in Season*. London: Hodder and Stoughton.

Schreiner, O. 1923a. *Thoughts on South Africa*. London: Unwin.

Schreiner, O. 1923b. *Stories, Dreams and Allegories: A New Edition in which is Included 'The Dawn of Civilisation' (Her Last Words, in 1920)*. London: Unwin.

Sedlar, J.W. 1980. *India and the Greek World: A Study in the Transmission of Culture*. Totowa, NJ: Rowman & Littlefield.

Sethia, T. & Narayan, A. (eds). 2013. *The Living Gandhi: Lessons for Our Times*. London: Penguin.

Smuts, J.C. 1926. *Holism and Evolution*. London: Macmillan.

Sorabji, R. 2012. *Gandhi and the Stoics: Modern Experiments on Ancient Values*. Oxford: Oxford University Press.

Stray, C. (ed). 2007. *Gilbert Murray Reassessed: Hellenism, Theatre, and International Politics*. Oxford: Oxford University Press.

Stray, C. 2014. 'Review of Edmund Richardson, *Classical Victorians: Scholars, Scoundrels and Generals in Pursuit of Antiquity. Classics after Antiquity*'. *BMCR* 5 June.

Swan, M. 1985. *Gandhi: The South African Experience*. Johannesburg: Ravan Press.

Tarn, W.W. 1951. *The Greeks in Bactria and India*. Cambridge: Cambridge University Press.

Thapar, R. 1990. *A History of India. Vol. I*. Baltimore: Penguin.

Tolstoy, L. 1930 (translated by Maude Aylmer, first published in 1897). *What is Art*? London: Oxford University Press (see page references in fn 33).
Tsuzuki, C. 1980. *Edward Carpenter 1844–1929: Prophet of Human Fellowship*. Cambridge: Cambridge University Press.
Vahed, G. 2000. '"African Gandhi": The South African War and the Limits of Imperial Identity'. *Historia* 45(1):201–19.
Vasunia, P. 2013. *The Classics and Colonial India*. Oxford: Oxford University Press.
West, F. 1984. *Gilbert Murray: A Life*. London: Palgrave Macmillan.
White, K.D. 1957. *Our Classical Tradition*. Johannesburg: SABC.
White, L.A. (ed). 1964. *Lewis Morgan*. Cambridge, MA: Harvard University Press.
Wiesehöfer, J. (ed). 2005. *Theodor Mommsen: Gelehrter, Politiker Und Literat*. Stuttgart: Franz Steiner.
Wilson, D. 1987. *Gilbert Murray O.M. 1866–1957*. Oxford: Clarendon Press.
Wood, E. 1981. 'Marxism and Ancient Greece'. *History Workshop* 11:3–22.

Gandhi and Socrates

Phiroze Vasunia

University College London

Gandhi composed his 'translation' of Plato's Apology *while he was in South Africa. Gandhi was responding to political restrictions against the Indian community and was also influenced by John Ruskin's* Unto This Last. *Interestingly, the translation was banned by the British authorities in India. This article explores the background to Gandhi's translation and examines the role of Plato's work in the development of his idea of* satyagraha.

Mohandas Gandhi first came to think of Socrates as a *satyagrahi* in South Africa. Gandhi read Plato's *Apology* while he was serving a jail sentence in Johannesburg in early 1908; he rendered the *Apology* into Gujarati, later in the same year, and published the Gujarati version across several instalments in *Indian Opinion*. The South African years have been extensively studied, of course, and numerous commentators have discussed the important place they hold in Gandhi's life. These years (1893–1914) were significant for his development as a political activist and philosopher of *satyagraha*, and indeed these were the years when he began to formulate his conception of Indian nationalism. Gandhi was himself to say later that he discovered his 'vocation in life' (Gandhi 1928:509) in South Africa and that he 'was born in India but was made in South Africa' (*CW* 84:380). As we try to understand Gandhi's 'story' of Socrates, we should bear in mind the South African context and the evolution that Gandhi underwent there as a political thinker. Over the course of his life, Gandhi appears to have read Plato's dialogues, a few works by Aristotle, and a few books on Greek philosophy, but he read voluminously in general and had no special interest in the ancient Greeks. In Socrates, he had an abiding interest, and it was in South Africa that he first began to identify with the Athenian philosopher.

It was in South Africa, moreover, that Gandhi read a book that had an even more powerful impact on him than the *Apology*, namely, *Unto This Last*, by John Ruskin. The book was given to him by Henry Polak, in 1904, and Gandhi famously read it in one sitting on the train from Johannesburg to Durban, rising 'with the dawn, ready to reduce these principles to practice' (*CW* 39:239). The 'conversion experience' that followed from a reading of this work prompted

Gandhi to write a Gujarati version, which he titled *Sarvodaya*, a word which could be translated roughly as 'the uplift of all' or 'the advancement of all'. The preface (*prastavana*) to the Gujarati version of *Sarvodaya*, which began to appear in *Indian Opinion* soon after the last instalment of Gandhi's version of the *Apology*, explicitly connected Ruskin to Socrates:

> Socrates gave us some idea of man's duty. He practised his precepts. It can be argued that Ruskin's ideas are an elaboration of Socrates's. Ruskin has described vividly how one who wants to live by Socrates's ideas should acquit himself in the different vocations. (*CW* 8:241)

One could scarcely argue with the first half of this analysis, and the latter half is arguably consistent with some views ascribed to Socrates, but Gandhi's remarks in general raise a question: in what way could Ruskin's book be seen as an extension of Socrates' words?

Gandhi's interpretation of Ruskin is notoriously eccentric, and scholarly readers have not fully accepted the reading that Gandhi puts forward in his *Autobiography*. But Kathryn Tidrick has reminded us about the important elements of 'self-sacrifice, even unto death,' that Gandhi discerned in *Unto This Last* (Tidrick 2006:68). If the good of the individual lay in the good of all, as Gandhi said, the individual might need to make the ultimate sacrifice and lay down his or her life for the benefit of society. This readiness to die for the community was almost a sacred duty, and it was a duty that Ruskin himself alluded to in *Unto This Last*.

> The fact is, that people never have had clearly explained to them the true functions of a merchant with respect to other people. I should like the reader to be very clear about this.
>
> Five great intellectual professions, relating to daily necessities of life, have hitherto existed – three exist necessarily, in every civilized nation:
> The Soldier's profession is to *defend* it.
> The Pastor's to *teach* it.
> The Physician's to *keep it in health.*
> The Lawyer's to *enforce justice* in it.
> The Merchant's to *provide* for it.
>
> And the duty of all these men is, on due occasion, to *die* for it.
> 'On due occasion,' namely: –
> The Soldier, rather than leave his post in battle.
> The Physician, rather than leave his post in plague.
> The Pastor, rather than teach Falsehood.
> The Lawyer, rather than countenance Injustice.
> The Merchant – what is *his* "due occasion" of death?
>
> It is the main question for the merchant, as for all of us. For, truly, the man who does not know when to die, does not know how to live. (Cook & Wedderburn 1905:39–40)

Since Gandhi was from a *bania* or merchant community and had studied law in London, he was arguably both a lawyer and a merchant and thus was familiar with two of the 'five great intellectual professions'. As a lawyer, Gandhi found no rest in South Africa and was constantly agitating for the rights of Indians and others. In these pages of *Unto This Last*, Ruskin was nonetheless interested in the merchant more than the lawyer: he wrote that the merchant ought to be ready to suffer on behalf of his men and even to suffer more than his men; the merchant or manufacturer should give of himself 'as a father would in a famine, shipwreck, or battle, sacrifice himself for his son' (Cook & Wedderburn 1905:45). In effect, Ruskin was showing Gandhi that a merchant could be a 'hero and martyr' if he were prepared to act in a spirit of self-sacrifice (Tidrick 2006:69).

But Ruskin mentions the soldier, pastor and physician as well as the lawyer and merchant in his list of five great intellectual professions, and we might also think of the affinity between Gandhi and the first group. In relation to the pastor, it is not difficult to point to passages in Gandhi's writings, even at this early date, where he speaks of his religious and spiritual convictions and offers people advice on religious, spiritual and moral issues. The Socrates of Gandhi's *Apology* speaks at times as if he were a preacher or as if he had an especially close connection to the divine. Nor is it difficult to think of Gandhi as a healer and physician, despite the scepticism he expresses about conventional 'western' medicine. In the preface to his version of the *Apology*, he writes that the Indian body politic is diseased. 'When the disease is diagnosed and its true nature revealed in public, and when, through suitable remedies, the body [politic] of India is cured and cleansed both within and without, it will become immune to the germs of the disease, that is, to the oppression by the British and the others.' Readers can find 'in the words of a great soul [Gandhi uses a form of *mahatma*] like Socrates the qualities of an elixir' (*CW* 8:174). When they have drunk this elixir, or *amrit*, Gandhi's readers may be able to fight off the disease and cure the afflicted body. Gandhi/Socrates is a special kind of physician who will help his followers and disciples overcome the moral sickness that restricts their spiritual growth and hinders their intellectual development.

Ruskin also places the soldier in the five professions he mentions in *Unto This Last*, and it is interesting to see Gandhi, the professor of non-violence, give prominence to the soldier, or warrior, in the heading under which he offers his version of the *Apology*. The title that he uses is *Ek satyavirni katha*, which can be translated as 'Story of a true soldier' or 'Story of a soldier of truth', the latter being the form employed in the English edition of the *Collected Works*. 'True soldier' is arguably more martial than 'soldier of truth', but in any case the association of Socrates with 'soldier' in Gandhi's version suggests that he thinks of Socrates as a figure who is ready to go to battle and to give up his life for what he knows to be the truth. Gandhi's Socrates is religious and pious, a man who says he believes in God, and a philosopher who has a soldier's toughness to withstand the hostility that he encounters in many quarters. Rather than choose words or terms that might connect Socrates simply or uniquely to a philosophical, spiritual or religious tradition, Gandhi refers to the Athenian as a *satyavir* and by that expression emphasises his willingness to fight unto death for his cause.

By making a soldier a part of his title, Gandhi may also be recalling the terms used by Plato in his *Apology*. Socrates uses military language to describe his own pursuit of philosophy in the face of threats to his wellbeing; he suggests that when he stands fast at his trial and declines to run away he is acting like a solider at his post; and he also implies that his own obedience to god is comparable to the obedience of the soldier to his commanding officer. In Henry Cary's (1905) translation, Socrates says:

> I should then be acting strangely, O Athenians, if, when the generals whom you chose to command me assigned me my post at Potidaea, at Amphipolis, and at Delium, I then remained where they posted me, like any other person, and encountered the danger of death, but when the deity as I thought and believed, assigned it as my duty to pass my life in the study of philosophy, and in examining myself and others, I should on that occasion, through fear of death or any thing else whatsoever, desert my post. (*Apology* 28d–29a)

Following Socrates, Gandhi is reframing the figure of the soldier or warrior and reclaiming him for his own particular cause and struggle.

Solider, physician, pastor, lawyer and merchant: Gandhi had affinities with all five and discerned in Ruskin's prose the exhortation to give up his own life if that were required of him. This emphasis on martyrdom and death is arguably even stronger in Gandhi's version of the *Apology* than in Plato's text. Gandhi writes in his preface that Socrates 'had no fear of death' and he goes on to describe the last moments of the Athenian philosopher. We are told about the hemlock that he administers to himself and the speech that he delivers in the presence of Phaedo. Gandhi adds, 'It is said that up to the very last moment Socrates showed no fear, and that he took the poison smilingly. As he finished the last sentence of his discourse, he drank the poison from the cup as eagerly as we might drink sherbet from a glass.' Socrates was 'a great satyagrahi' and a role-model to Indians in the subcontinent as well as in South Africa: 'We must learn to live and die like Socrates.' Gandhi urges his readers not to be afraid and not to act out of 'fear of dishonour or death' and to grasp the true nature of the problems afflicting Indian society and culture.

While Gandhi omits or condenses other parts of the *Apology*, he affords his readers a fuller view of Socrates' remarks on death. We are reminded of Socrates' views on death in the last three of the six instalments that Gandhi published in *Indian Opinion*. The sixth and final instalment, in particular, begins with a statement by the editor (Gandhi) saying that he had mistakenly announced the end of the serialisation of the *Apology* the previous week. Gandhi notes that Socrates was found guilty by a majority of the jurors and he then offers a translation of the remarks made by the Athenian after the vote and the award of the death penalty. Gandhi ends the instalment by insisting on the historicity of the trial and defence of Socrates:

> We pray to God, and want our readers also to pray, that they, and we too, may have the moral strength which enabled Socrates to follow virtue to the end and to embrace

> death as if it were his beloved. We advise everyone to turn his mind again and again to Socrates' words and conduct. (*CW* 8:229)

Gandhi doubtless had several reasons for not wanting to leave his rendition of the *Apology* incomplete, but the reference to death in these passages would have certainly been a factor in his decision to finish the job. Bearing in mind that Plato composed his dialogue in Greek, let us set down here an excerpt from the sixth instalment in the Gujarati of Gandhi (Figure 1) and in the English translation of the *Collected Works*. Let us, for the sake of comparison, also set down the parallel passage in the translation by Henry Cary. Gandhi does not say which translation of Plato he read in jail in 1908, but he is likely to have read the *Defence and Death of Socrates*, which was a small book that contained only the *Apology* and part of the *Phaedo* in Cary's translation. (The list of authorities appended to *Hind Swaraj*, a text in dialogue form which Gandhi wrote in 1909, includes the '"Defence and Death of Socrates" – from Plato'.) Cary published his translations of Plato in the 19th century; the *Defence* was printed in 1905 and distributed in South Africa as well as in Britain.

Gandhi uses forms of the noun *maut* (for the English 'death') frequently in this passage, although elsewhere he also uses *mrityu*, and we can see that he deploys

CW 8:228:

In any case, I have only a few years left to live. You could not be troubled to wait and you have earned an evil name for yourselves by condemning an innocent man to death. If you had waited a while, I would have died in the course of nature, for I am an old man, far advanced in years. If I had used ignoble arguments before you and adopted the course common on such occasions, I would have escaped the death penalty. But that would have been inconsistent with my duty. I am sure a free man will never do anything unworthy of himself to save himself from death or other danger. One ought not to try to save oneself from death by any and every means. In battle, a man can save himself by laying down his arms and surrendering to the enemy. But we think such a man a coward. In the same way, anyone who resorts to unscrupulous means to save himself from death is an unworthy person. I think it is more difficult to save oneself from wickedness than from death, for wickedness is swifter than death.

Cary 1905:38–40:

For the sake of no long space of time, O Athenians, you will incur the character and reproach at the hands of those who wish to defame the city, of having put that wise man, Socrates, to death. For those who wish to defame you will assert that I am wise, though I am not. If, then, you had waited for a short time, this would have happened of its own accord; for observe my age, that it is far advanced in life, and near death. But I say this not to you all, but to those only who have condemned me to die. And I say this, too, to the same persons.
Perhaps you think, O Athenians, that I have been convicted through the want of arguments, by which I might have persuaded you, had I thought it right to do and say any thing, so that I might escape punishment. Far otherwise: I have been convicted through want indeed, yet not of arguments, but of audacity and impudence, and of the inclination to say such things to you as would have been most agreeable for you to hear, had I lamented and bewailed and done and said many other things unworthy of me, as I affirm, but such as you are accustomed to hear from others.

Being impatient and rash, you have taken a step which spells wickedness – wickedness which is so swift in its advance. You have sentenced me to death. I shall now leave this world. My opponents will be looked upon as men who betrayed truth and perpetrated an injustice. I will suffer my punishment. But they will [also] suffer the penalty for their [evil] deeds. This is what always happens. Perhaps it is just as well that it should be so.

But neither did I then think that I ought, for the sake of avoiding danger, to do any thing unworthy of a freeman, nor do I now repent of having so defended myself; but I should much rather choose to die, having so defended myself, than to live in that way. For neither in a trial nor in battle is it right that I or any one else should employ every possible means whereby he may avoid death; for in battle it is frequently evident that a man might escape death by laying down his arms, and throwing himself on the mercy of his pursuers. And there are many other devices in every danger, by which to avoid death, if a man dares to do and say every thing. But this is not difficult, O Athenians, to escape death; but it is much more difficult to avoid depravity, for it runs swifter than death. And now I, being slow and aged, am overtaken by the slower of the two; but my accusers, being strong and active, have been overtaken by the swifter, wickedness.

And now I depart, condemned by you to death; but they condemned by truth, as guilty of iniquity and injustice: and I abide my sentence, and so do they. These things, perhaps, ought so to be, and I think that they are for the best.

the term in order to give prominence to Socrates' attitude to death and to his execution. In Gujarati as in English, Gandhi is more terse than Cary and he keeps the focus on the jurors' decision and Socrates' response to death. Socrates is innocent, he is old, he acts in a manner that is consistent with his own principles, and he is prepared to meet death worthily rather than run away from it in a

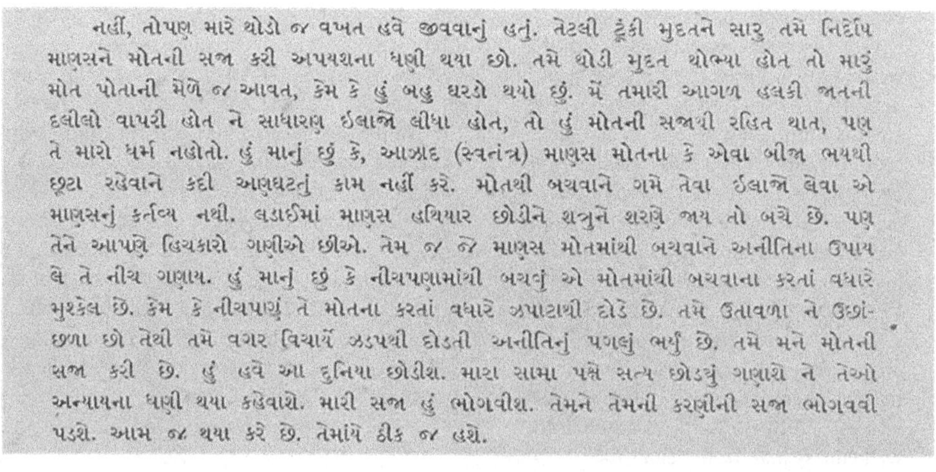

નહીં, તોપણ મારે થોડો જ વખત હવે જીવવાનું હતું. તેટલી ટૂંકી મુદતને સારુ તમે નિર્દોષ માણસને મોતની સજા કરી અપયશના ધણી થયા છો. તમે થોડી મુદત થોભ્યા હોત તો મારું મોત પોતાની મેળે જ આવત, કેમ કે હું બહુ ઘરડો થયો છું. મેં તમારી આગળ હલકી જાતની દલીલો વાપરી હોત ને સાધારણ ઈલાજો લીધા હોત, તો હું મોતની સજાથી રહિત થાત, પણ તે મારો ધર્મ નહોતો. હું માનું છું કે, આઝાદ (સ્વતંત્ર) માણસ મોતના કે એવા બીજા ભયથી છૂટા રહેવાને કદી અણઘટતું કામ નહીં કરે. મોતથી બચવાને ગમે તેવા ઈલાજો લેવા એ માણસનું કર્તવ્ય નથી. લડાઈમાં માણસ હથિયાર છોડીને શત્રુને શરણે જાય તો બચે છે. પણ તેને આપણે હિચકારો ગણીએ છીએ. તેમ જ જે માણસ મોતમાંથી બચવાને અનીતિના ઉપાય લે તે નીચ ગણાય. હું માનું છું કે નીચપણામાંથી બચવું એ મોતમાંથી બચવાના કરતાં વધારે મુશ્કેલ છે. કેમ કે નીચપણું તે મોતના કરતાં વધારે ઝપાટાથી દોડે છે. તમે ઉતાવળા ને ઉછાંછળા છો તેથી તમે વગર વિચાર્યે ઝડપથી દોડતી અનીતિનું પગલું ભર્યું છે. તમે મને મોતની સજા કરી છે. હું હવે આ દુનિયા છોડીશ. મારા સામા પક્ષે સત્ય છોડ્યું ગણાશે ને તેઓ અન્યાયના ધણી થયા કહેવાશે. મારી સજા હું ભોગવીશ. તેમને તેમની કરણીની સજા ભોગવવી પડશે. આમ જ થયા કરે છે. તેમાંયે ઠીક જ હશે.

Figure 1. *Indian Opinion* 9 May 1908. (In *Gandhijino akshardeha* 8:218)

cowardly fashion. His opponents are bloodthirsty; they seek an old man's death; they are reckless, wicked and unjust. Cary's translation conveys something of this sensibility, but perhaps also gives the reader a sense of the philosopher's interest in wisdom and rational argument. Cary does not stray far from Plato's Greek. Yet, Gandhi in the Gujarati does wander from Cary's English, and one of the interesting points about Gandhi's rendition in this and other passages that touch on the issue of death is precisely that by his excisions he amplifies the emphasis on death. That Socrates is happy to lay down his life in the right way, for the right reason, and at the right time is a message that Gandhi takes to heart and strives to put across to his readers.

In claiming that Ruskin's *Unto This Last* is a reading of the *Apology*, Gandhi is, I think, reminding us of Ruskin's emphasis on duty and self-sacrifice and the spiritual obligation to commit one's life to the cause of equality. Socrates' speech in the *Apology* has no overt connection with the political economy discussed extensively by Ruskin in his work. Ruskin derived the title of his book from chapter 20 of Matthew in the New Testament. When some labourers point out to a householder that they have worked for longer hours than the workers who arrived at his vineyard later in the day, the householder says that he will pay the last man the same amount of money as the first: 'Friend, I do thee no wrong: didst not thou agree with me for a penny? Take that thine is, and go thy way: I will give unto this last, even as unto thee.' There is, in Plato's *Apology*, no trace of this parable, or of Ruskinian socialism, or indeed of an ethic that might have guided the founding of Tolstoy Farm. We might surmise that, with his paraphrase of the *Apology*, Gandhi retains the ambiguity in Ruskin's title and interprets it not just in the terms of equal pay to all workers but also in the terms of a principled commitment to be upheld to the very end of one's life, that is, unto the last or unto death. Gandhi is certainly aware of the Biblical significance of the phrase and observes in his version of *Unto This Last* that he employs the title *Sarvodaya*, rather than a literal translation, since the expression from the New Testament will 'be understood only by a person who has read the Bible in English' (*CW* 8:241). It is notable in this context that Socrates was commonly seen as a Christ figure in the 19th century and earlier and that Gandhi's Socrates bears some similarities to Christ. Gandhi may have absorbed the parallels drawn between Christ and Socrates in the course of his readings in London and South Africa. Perhaps not incidentally, Gandhi in his later years was compared to both Christ and Socrates.

The emphasis on death in the *Apology*, however, need not be taken to refer to some sort of naive or starry-eyed outlook on the part of Gandhi. He may have been deeply influenced by 'a Jain-inflected Hindu orthodoxy and late Victorian psychomancy, the world of Madame Blavatsky, Theosophy, *planchette*, and the Esoteric Christian Union', but he was also uncannily successful in his dealings with political opponents (Anderson 2012:19). Both his South African and his British opponents were unnerved by the moral certainty and conviction that he showed in his dealings with them, and they would have been rattled by the notion that they were dealing with an activist who was prepared to wage his battle unto the last breath. Jail sentences scarcely troubled him, and he wrote in 1922, that 'the prison cell where Socrates drank the poison cup was undoubtedly the way to bliss' (*CW* 22:245).

Besides, although Gandhi wrote his version of the *Apology* before he threw himself fully into the independence movement in India, he had already begun to develop the concept of *satyagraha*, and it is possible to see in his words nascent support for those Indians who were, literally and otherwise, soldiers in the war against British colonialism. As Ajay Skaria observes:

> ... the heroic nationalists who gave their life to the nation also practiced a certain living by dying, where they gave themselves to their very death for a cause. This very giving of themselves to their death authorized a living on and an evading of death so that their cause, the nation, could be better pursued. (2010:217)

Gandhi's rendering of the *Apology* is, in this sense, consistent with the behaviour of anti-colonial nationalists and it clarifies their actions.

Gandhi's attitudes to death and mortality were also part of a complicated if mostly consistent spiritual and political programme. This programme evolved somewhat over the course of Gandhi's life, was shaped by such things as his experience of religion, Indian diaspora communities, and colonialism, and nurtured *satyagraha* and *ahimsa*, with their distinctively Gandhian attributes. Gandhi's willingness to accept death was intimately connected to his philosophy, to his way of being in the world, and in particular to the principles of *ahimsa* and *satyagraha* that he espoused and followed until the end (Skaria 2010; Sorabji 2012).

The initial context of publication also explains why Gandhi's *Ek satyavirni katha* becomes a vehicle for civil disobedience from an early date. I have touched on some of the circumstances above, but it is worth noting that the instalments appeared in *Indian Opinion*, a bilingual (initially, multilingual) English and Gujarati newspaper that was, at the same time, not a newspaper in the conventional sense of the word (Hofmeyr 2013). In the issue[1] that contained the sixth instalment of Gandhi's *Apology*, *Indian Opinion* ran articles or editorials on government Bills that affected the rights of Indians in the region; the colour question; the poll tax; the 'Asiatic Question'; 'Asiatic Passive Resistance'; and 'A Progressive Indian', to name a few topics. As these examples show, *Indian Opinion* was concerned with the predicament of Indian immigrants around the Empire and took a stand against racial injustice and political oppression, especially when these affected Indians. The newspaper informed the Indian diaspora community in South Africa but was also, in its overseas location, contributing to an evolving sense of Indian nationhood (Devji 2012). Moreover, the International Printing Press, which printed the newspaper, additionally published pamphlets and items from the newspaper and then distributed these separately to readers in South Africa and India: one of these pamphlets was none other than the translation of Plato that we have been considering. Gandhi's interpretation of the *Apology* was thus part of a print culture in which moral teachings and political demands existed side-by-side with sundry translations, reportage, and reflections on India, the British Empire, South Africa, and race.

The Gandhian provenance of Plato's *Apology* made it suspect in the eyes of the British authorities, who, in 1910, banned the pamphlet in Bombay. According to a notice in *The Bombay Government Gazette*,[2] the translation of the *Apology* was seized by officers since it deployed 'words which are likely to bring into hatred and contempt the Government established by law in British India and to excite disaffection to the said Government'. These expressions were formulaic and evoked the strictures of the Press Act of 1910. The *Gazette* also disclosed that three other works were banned by the government, namely, *Hind Swaraj*, *Sarvodaya*, and a copy of a speech delivered by Mustafa Kamal Pasha. The last was a reference to a speech given by Mustafa Kamal in October 1907, in Alexandria, a few months before his death, which occurred, in February 1908, in Cairo. Gandhi, who was sympathetic to the Egyptian, had translated the speech into Gujarati and published it in *Indian Opinion* in June 1908.[3] The text of Plato's *Apology* now belonged to a literature that, in the language of the Press Act, contained 'words, signs or visible representations which are likely or may have a tendency, directly or indirectly, whether by inference, suggestion, allusion, metaphor, implication or otherwise' to threaten the British government of India.

The inclusion of a translation of Plato's *Apology* in the list of banned works was slightly anomalous in so far as it is the only one of the four that went back to antiquity. Clearly, the source of the publication and the identity of the 'translator' set off alarm bells in the British administration. Gandhi's version was not the first translation of the *Apology* into an Indian language; it was not even the first version into Gujarati. Ala al-Din Sharif Salih Muhammad published the second edition of his Gujarati account of Socrates – which admittedly draws on various dialogues by Plato and not just the *Apology* – in Bombay as early as 1897.[4] Indian treatments of Greek philosophy were permitted to circulate by the colonial authorities (for example the Urdu discussion of Ihsan Allah published in 1883), as were other translations of Plato. In Gandhi's lifetime, the British administrator Frank Lugard Brayne wrote *Socrates in an Indian Village* and a series of related titles as part of his programme of rural development in the Punjab. In 1931, more strikingly, Sir John Gilbert Laithwaite, a British civil servant and later private secretary to the Viceroy, wrote a pseudo-Platonic dialogue between Socrates and Gandhi, for the entertainment of another civil servant, Sir (Samuel) Findlater Stewart, the permanent under secretary of state for India.[5] It was not Socrates or Plato who troubled the officers of the British government in India; it was Gandhi's portrayal of Socrates that was the source of the grievance.

The notice in the *Bombay Government Gazette* did not pass unremarked on by Gandhi, who responded with a short piece in *Indian Opinion*[6] and pointed out that the '*Defence of Socrates* or *The Story of a True Warrior* is a Gujarati rendering of Plato's immortal work printed in order to illustrate the virtue and the true nature of passive resistance'. He also wrote that the banned publications, with the exception of *Hind Swaraj*, had been with the reading public for some time. These publications, Gandhi writes, 'are intended to impart a lofty, moral tone to the reader and are, in our opinion, works capable of being put into children's hands without any danger whatsoever'. The government was trying 'to stop the circulation of literature that shows the slightest independence of spirit' and was likely to be consumed by excessive zeal. Gandhi goes on to present himself and his associates as champions of passive resistance and maintains that they will not be affected by the government's repression. He agrees with the authorities that violence is unacceptable and adds that 'the only way we know to eradicate the disease is to popularize passive resistance of the right stamp. Any other way, especially repression, must inevitably fail in the long run' (*CW* 10:245).

By the time Gandhi returned to India from South Africa, Socrates was established in his mind as the exemplar of a *satyagrahi*. When the Rowlatt Act of 1919 took aim at the possession of seditious documents, the Satyagraha Sabha, led by Gandhi, decided to disseminate the same four tracts, including the Gujarati translation of Plato's *Apology*, that were banned for sedition in 1910. As one critic notes, 'the rereading and translation of the *Apology* becomes one of the first acts of civil disobedience for the 1919 *satyagraha*' (Gandhi 1996–1997:120). The statement by the Sabha noted that the books had been selected since they were 'not inconsistent with satyagraha, and ... therefore, of a clean type and ... [did] not, either directly or indirectly, approve of or encourage violence' (*CW* 15:192). In the Congress Report on the subsequent unrest in the Punjab, Gandhi again expounded on the meaning of *satyagraha* as truth-force and observed that Socrates was a *satyagrahi* since he insisted on telling the truth to young Athenians and then laid down his life for that principle (*CW* 17:152–3). *Satyagraha* was non-violent and involved self-control, he added, and it could not be blamed for the violence and pillaging of the protesters in the Punjab.

'There was once a wise man, named Socrates, who lived in Athens. His unconventional ideas, which, however, spread love of truth and goodness, displeased the authorities, and he was sentenced to death' (*CW* 49:169). As the letter to a relative confirms, Gandhi's identification with Socrates persisted at least into the 1930s, when he again summarised the *Apology*, though far more briefly this time. Yet, it is a mistake to extrapolate from Gandhi's references to truth and goodness in his writings on Socrates and to think of him as a simple, unsophisticated, or overly literal reader of Greek philosophy. Plato and Socrates are not the first names that come to mind in connection with anti-colonialism or civil disobedience or with spiritual renewal, but one of the interesting features of the engagement with Socrates, in South Africa and India, is how Gandhi 'brings to insurgency' the words of a Platonic text (Gandhi 1996–1997:120). This reading of Socrates was not entirely new and took its inspiration from, among other things, the writings of Ruskin and 19th-century conceptions of Socrates as a martyr. Ruskin, in particular, had awoken in Gandhi a powerful understanding of Plato's text and affirmed for him that the struggle for *satyagraha* needed to be upheld at all costs, unto the last, even unto death. Many of Gandhi's interlocutors, opponents and gaolers would have had a far deeper knowledge than Gandhi of Plato's Greek and a more wide-ranging familiarity with Plato's dialogues (and, for that matter, of Ruskin's work). Gandhi could not read classical Greek. But it was he, and not they, who perceived the transformative potential of the *Apology* in an English translation of the Victorian period and who thereby came to a better understanding of *satyagraha*, the truth-force that brought an Empire to its knees.

Acknowledgement

I am grateful to Isabel Hofmeyr, Javed Majeed and the journal's readers for their help with this article.

Notes

1. 9 May 1908.
2. 24 March 1910, no 12, part I:442.
3. See *Indian Opinion* 27 June 1908; *CW* 8:326.
4. *Pletonan prasnottara* 2nd edition, Bombay.
5. British Library, India Office Records, MSS Eur/F138/171.
6. 7 May 1910.

References

Allah, I. 1883. *Tarikh i Hukama i Yunan*. Gorakhpur.

Anderson, P. 2012. *The Indian Ideology*. Gurgaon: Three Essays.

Cary, H. (trans). 1905. *The Defence and Death of Socrates*. London: Arthur C. Field.

Cook, E.T. & Wedderburn, A. (eds). 1905. *The Works of John Ruskin* vol 17. London: George Allen.

Devji, F. 2012. *The Impossible Indian: Gandhi and the Temptations of Violence*. London: Hurst & Company.

Gandhi, M.K. 1869–1948. *The Collected Works of Mahatma Gandhi* [*CW*] 100 volumes. Delhi: Publications Division: Ministry of Information and Broadcasting, India.

Gandhi, M.K. 1928. *Satyagraha in South Africa* (V.G. Desai trans). Madras: S. Ganesan.

Gandhi, L. 1996–1997. 'Concerning Violence: The Limits and Circulations of Gandhian Ahimsa or Passive Resistance'. *Cultural Critique* 35:105–147.

Hofmeyr, I. 2013. *Gandhi's Printing Press: Experiments in Slow Reading*. Cambridge, MA: Harvard University Press.

Majeed, J. 2007. *Autobiography, Travel and Postnational Identity: Gandhi, Nehru and Iqbal*. Houndmills, Basingstoke: Palgrave Macmillan.

Skaria, A. 2010. 'Living by Dying', in A. Pandian & D. Ali (eds), *Ethical Life in South Asia*. Bloomington: Indiana University Press.

Sorabji, R. 2012. *Gandhi and the Stoics: Modern Experiments on Ancient Values*. Oxford: Oxford University Press.

Tidrick, K. 2006. *Gandhi: A Political and Spiritual Life*. London: I.B. Tauris.

English in India and South Africa: Comparisons, Commonalities and Contrasts

Rajend Mesthrie

University of Cape Town

This article offers a comparison of the history of English in India and South Africa, with special reference to its rise as a second language. As far as external history is concerned both territories show investment in a language whose use has long outlasted the colonial era, despite the concerns of leaders and scholars with a pro-indigenous language stance. The article focuses on comparing the grammatical characteristics of the second language varieties of English in India and South Africa, arising from the Mouton World Atlas of Variation in English. *A comparison of relevant chapters in this work reveals close structural similarities between Indian English and Black South African English. Moreover, South African Indian English falls midway between the two in this typological survey.*

Linguistically, India and South Africa share the obvious heritage of British colonialism, which made English a language of government, administration, education and societal aspirations to varying degrees. In both territories indigenous languages (and their speakers) proved resilient in resisting shift to the colonial language, forming instead a relatively balanced multilingualism (unlike the dominion territories of the United States, Canada, Australia and New Zealand). There is accordingly much to be gained by making linguistic comparisons between the English of indigenous people in India and South Africa. A second strand of the India-South Africa connection concerns the English of Indian South Africans (or SAIE). Unlike the two varieties cited above, it became the home language of almost the entire million-strong Indian community of South Africa within a century and a quarter of the first arrival of Indians in Port Natal in 1860. The links between SAIE and Indian English (henceforth IE) are strong because of direct historical connections (for example teachers and interpreters from India – see Brain 1983; Badassy 2002) as well as common substrate languages (Hindi, Bhojpuri, Tamil, Telugu, Gujarati and Konkani in South Africa – see Mesthrie 2002). But there are differences too, arising out of the ethos of indenture and petty trading in South Africa, and the relatively rapid stabilisation as a home language.

Models of Postcolonial English

The English language is today best seen as a 'complex' made up of many different types, depending on a three-way distinction between English as a native language (ENL), English as a second language (ESL) and English as a foreign language (EFL). These days this trichotomy is visualised more dynamically in terms of Braj Kachru's (1988) model of an Inner Circle, Outer Circle and Expanding Circle. Inner Circle countries have English as a mother tongue (L1 or first language) spoken by a majority: the examples are Britain and the dominion countries of colonisation (US, Canada, Australia, New Zealand, South Africa and Newfoundland). In these colonies was often wrought the destruction of indigenous languages, directly or, more often, indirectly. English in the Outer Circle is the result of a defining encounter with British colonialism, which installed it as an official language of administration and education. In such territories (like Kenya, Nigeria, Malaysia and Sri Lanka) local languages remained robust, and English was spoken by a minority as a second language, growing in time into an important element of local politics and administration that would outlast the colonial era. The Expanding Circle is conceived of as a group of territories in which there was no significant British colonial presence, the English language hence being foreign, and little used for internal communication or nation-building. Implicit in the model is the notion that English has nevertheless been an important language for international communication and for keeping abreast of Anglo-American science and technologies in Expanding Circle countries like Japan, South Korea and Norway. The complications of the model in relation to English-based Creoles, new hybridities that include code-switching, code-mixing, globalisation and new electronic media will not be discussed, as they are of less relevance to this historically-based, comparative survey. India is usually taken as prototypically ESL terrain, with the number of speakers of British English significantly diminished after independence. Nevertheless, the role of English has grown, although always in tandem with one or more local languages. The English of educated Indian elites has in fact sparked an important debate within linguistics of the ontological status of the native speaker. Scholars like Rama Kant Agnihotri and Rajendra Singh (2012) have pointed to a monolingual bias in western conceptions of linguistic nativeness (especially after Noam Chomsky 1965). They stress that in multilingual societies an individual's expertise is spread over more than one language, an investment that results in a complementary and cumulative expertise in a set of languages, rather than in a single, first-learned language.

South Africa has always posed a problem for international models of English. It began as a dominion territory, in which the establishment of a large settler community would have made it something of an Inner Circle country. On the other hand, the proportion of the Settler strand of English speakers in relation to the indigenous population was not as great as in other dominion territories. The resilience of the indigenous population and the Bantu languages in particular made English decidedly a second language for the majority in South Africa.[1] Language shift to English remains uncommon, unlike the situation with the indigenous populations in all the other dominion territories. Colonial and apartheid separations further pushed the country into two linguistic realms, at least within the 'Circles' model – it was both Inner and Outer Circle. There was also the complication of Afrikaans as a second competing language of power in the 20th century.

Two other models are of relevance to the comparison of English in India and South Africa. The first concerns the historian's distinction between trade colonies, exploitation colonies, and colonies of settlement, which was introduced into contact linguistics by Salikoko Mufwene (2001). Strictly speaking, India would have been an exploitation colony, at best a 'company state' (Metcalf & Metcalf 2006:68), with British employees of the East India company preferring to send their children 'home' for their education, and to return to Britain themselves on retirement. Dominion territories like South Africa encouraged a settler mode with free enterprise, and a colonial system of education. This meant a larger presence of mother-tongue speakers of English, including young children, with greater possibilities for the spread of English as a colloquial second language.

The 'dynamic model' of Edgar Schneider (2003, 2007) posits a similar trajectory in terms of five stages based on constant relationships and communication needs in colonial and postcolonial territories: a 'foundation' stage of initial contact; an 'exonormative' orientation towards British English; a 'nativisation' phase as new localised norms start to develop; subsequent acceptance of an 'endonormative' colonial variety; and finally, postcolonial differentiation. By Schneider's model both India and South Africa are in stage 4: India shows 'early symptoms' of phase 4 (2007:171), while South Africa moved into phase 4 with its rainbow unity of 1994 onwards (2007:185).

Comparative Historical Background

As far as English in India is concerned, Kachru (1983:18–22) identified four key early periods: initial trade and reconnaissance (1600 onwards), missionary activity (1659 onwards), local demand (Rammohun Roy's petition of 1823 and onwards), and government policy (Macaulay's minute of 1825). Whereas the East India Company had initially supported an 'Orientalist' position with colleges of education in Sanskrit and Arabic, an 'Anglicist' movement stressed the need for western education and the English language. The Anglicists gained the upper hand after Macaulay's influential minute of 1835, with government schools being established in the major cities (Metcalf & Metcalf 2006:83; see also Sedlatschek 2009:xx).

There are broad parallels in southern Africa, with some exceptions. A significant presence of English began in the Cape in 1795, with a civilian rather than a transient military or administrative presence from 1820 on. The need for English as a lingua franca was staved off somewhat by the presence of Afrikaans in parts of the country and the development of Fanakalo pidgin in the early 19th century, with its largely Zulu-based vocabulary and its basic, non-Zulu grammar (Mesthrie 1989). Missionary activity from 1800 on was also important in developing literacy in indigenous languages and English, even if for a small number of 'mission elites'. While the growth of English and English-based education was always slow, it was further stunted by the policy of apartheid from 1948, which caused the withdrawal of English in social contexts by its enforced separation of racially defined groups. It also attempted to limit the influence of English in education. The ensuing schoolchildren's protests of 1976 in Soweto against the use of Afrikaans in the Bantu education system achieved the opposite, with English becoming the major language of education. Thus by the time of their respective independence from colonial rule, English had already consolidated its position in the school and university education systems of South Africa and India. In India too language-inspired protests (against Hindi in the South, especially in Tamil Nadu 1965) handed a further postcolonial advantage to English over other rivals (Hardgrave 1965). Overall political unity in both South Africa and India was achieved largely in the colonial language.

South Africa does not appear to have experienced an Anglicist versus Africanist controversy, with most scholars taking a pragmatic stance on English as a language of education in a multilingual context. The notable exception has been Neville Alexander (1989), whose ideas about socioeconomic and political empowerment included language as a crucial element of decolonisation and challenge to western hegemony. In many ways Alexander was an unwitting follower of Mohandas Gandhi on the language question (Mesthrie 1993). It was Gandhi who strongly called into question the position of English in pre-independence India's public life and education (Sinha 1978:153). The Gandhian influence resulted in numerous institutions being set up across India, which aimed at promoting indigenous education in the years before Independence (Mehrotra 1998:5). Mesthrie (1993) argues that Gandhi's thoughts on a language policy for India were based on his experiences of the multilingualism of South Africa's Indian community. As he notes in *Young India*[2] 'Little does anyone know that almost all Tamils and the Telugus in South Africa can carry on an intelligent conversation in Hindi'. Alexander's writings on language policy in South Africa were widely admired internationally, but do not appear to have struck a resonating chord within South Africa, outside of academic applied linguistics. Thus postcolonial India and South Africa remain on parallel tracks linguistically. In both territories indigenous languages continue to be spoken in large numbers (with the exception of South Africa's non-Bantu click languages, a.k.a. 'Khoe-San') and held in high esteem as languages of community, intimacy and solidarity, though not necessarily as languages of aspiration – especially educational aspirations. At the same time English has grown in stature as a lingua franca, as a language of education, politics, business, technology and creative writing. It is also a marker of a new middle-class elite who are multilingual, but speak English as a dominant language. Claudia Lange notes how English is becoming a colloquial (or 'vernacular') language in present-day India:

> English in India has never been a vernacular comparable to English in the US, and it has mostly been acquired in schools and universities rather than being transmitted from one generation to the next. It is probably only now, at the beginning of the new millenium, that something akin to an [Indian English] vernacular is developing. Political and social changes over the last three decades have contributed to the unprecedented rise of a large Indian middle class, urban and cosmopolitan, whose children will frequently grow up with English as part of their overall linguistic repertoire. Thus the dominance of a taught 'scholastic form' of English in India is now complemented by a truly vernacular [Indian English], as English has become a language of daily interaction for a still small, but growing number of the population. (2012:47)

This passage could have been written almost verbatim with the black middle classes of post-apartheid South Africa in mind, with the sole exception of the time period being closer to the 'last two' rather than three decades. Post-apartheid openness has in addition seen the crossing over of young middle-class speakers into the space that was once associated with prestige white accents. This new development in South African English, which I term a 'deracialisation' of the language, is beginning to exercise a fair amount of scholarship from the disciplines of sociolinguistics and education (see Mesthrie 2010a; McKinney 2013; Toefy 2014; Wilmot 2014). In addition to the specificities of Indian and South African developments, there is the common thread of the globalisation of English via the electronic media and their associated popular culture.

Notwithstanding these developments in the new middle classes, the older, more traditional variety of Black South African English (henceforth BSAE) continues to be used robustly among older speakers and young people lacking access to suburban schools. It has become *more* prominent on radio and television, parliament and public meetings than the erstwhile 'Inner Circle' variety. What follows in this article is a comparison of the linguistic features of this traditional variety of BSAE and IE, from which the usage of the most elite and least fluent are excluded. The extent to which South Africa's Indian community fits into this comparison will also be briefly considered, again from a linguistic rather than literary perspective.

Grammatical Comparisons

This section is concerned with exploring the broad similarities and differences between the 'mesolectal' or mid-range varieties spoken by Indians and black South Africans. Such mesolectal varieties are spoken fluently but would not necessarily be associated with the young, new elites. The main comparison will be in the areas of syntax and morphology, afforded by the recently completed *Mouton World Atlas of Variation* (Kortmann & Lunkenheimer 2012). A phonetic comparison is less likely to yield strong similarities. The differences between a mesolectal Indian and black South African accent are evident even to casual observers, but for reasons of space will not be treated here. Bernd Kortmann and Kerstin Lunkenheimer devised a questionnaire of 235 mainly syntactic features that showed some degree of variation in the Englishes of the world.

Their survey of 74 varieties included 18 ESL varieties, 30 regional varieties of L1 English and 26 English-based pidgins and Creoles.[3] The 235 features were divided into 12 sections as follows: I *Pronouns*; II *Noun phrase*; III *Tense and aspect*; IV *Modal verbs*; V *Verb morphology*; VI *Negation*; VII *Agreement*; VIII *Relativization*; IX *Complementation*; X *Adverbial subordination*; XI *Adverbs and prepositions*; XII *Discourse organization and word order*. The features analysed are the most common ones reported in the 'World Englishes' and English dialectology literature that differ from the grammar of standard English. Such features have come to be known as 'Angloversals' (Mair 2003). Specialists in the different varieties contributed to a questionnaire and provided an overview essay on each variety covered in the project. For the questionnaire they provided rating responses per individual item as follows: *obligatory or pervasive; neither pervasive nor extremely rare; extremely rare; absent; not applicable; no information available*. The questionnaire for India was filled by Devyani Sharma of Queen Mary College, while the present author was responsible for BSAE and SAIE. Some of these features are attributable to processes of simplification or over generalisation in second-language acquisition. Thus IE and BSAE have a similar tendency to use non-count nouns (i.e. collective, mass, or related abstract nouns) as if they are countable nouns (feature 55): examples include *hardwares, apparels* (IE) and *machineries, furnitures* (BSAE). Both varieties are known to extend the use of present progressive marking to habitual and stative contexts. Thus Sharma (2012:527) gives the IE example of *We are knowing each other*, while Mesthrie (2012a:498) gives the example of *People who are having time for their children* ... Both varieties use double conjunctions across clauses (feature 215) as in IE (*Though the farmer works hard, but he cannot produce enough*, see Nihalani, Tongue, Hosali & Crowther 2004:179) and BSAE *Although I'm not that shy, but it's hard for me to make friends* (Mesthrie 2012a:499). The fact that examples like these recur in other ESLs led early analysts to conclude that they are more likely to reflect general tendencies of second-language acquisition, rather than substrate influences from speakers' mother tongues. However, more recent research (for example Sharma 2009; Van Rooy 2014; Paulasto 2014) based on the availability of large computer-based corpora and data extraction tools is beginning to find subtle differences between ESLs amidst the broad similarities. In regard to the English of India and Singapore, Sharma shows that substrate influences, rather than universals of processing, are the main driving force for extension of the progressive and copula omission. Bertus van Rooy's detailed work on the progressive with extended temporal duration in BSAE uncovers influence from Bantu language persistative usage (see also Makalela 2004).

Substrate influences from local languages in India and South Africa are sometimes transparently evident, as may be seen in the phenomenon of reduplication (feature 40 – i.e. repetition of a word or morpheme for regular semantic effects like intensity, repetition, plurality, distribution etc). This is a regular feature of the grammar of North Indian languages which is very common in IE. Thus Sharma (2012:526) gives the example of *four-four* mangoes ('four mangoes each') and *slowly-slowly* 'very slowly'. Reduplication does not have this semantic effect in the Bantu languages of relevance here. Rather it has an attenuative semantics: thus Zulu *hamba* 'to travel' versus *hamba-hamba* 'to just travel along, to saunter'. This feature does not appear to have been transferred into BSAE: there is no mention of it in any of the current sources on this variety. One reason for this is a possible clash with informal L1 South African English forms in which reduplication has the 'intensity' or 'repetition' meaning in forms like *now-now* 'soon', *quick-quick* 'very quickly' etc. These forms are ultimately based on Afrikaans templates.

Of interest too are forms that are not purely grammatical, but carry cultural or pragmatic overtones. Politeness in grammar may be evoked by indirect forms of address, special pronoun forms, or special verb forms. A question once posed to me by a respectful child in Cape Town was *Does Uncle Rajend know that Uncle Rajend's cat likes to play with string?*, showing indirect forms of address for vocative as well as genitive.[4] These effects would account for non-standard uses of modal auxiliaries like BSAE *May you please attend to this matter*, in which the polite first person standard form of *may* is generalised to the second person (feature 127, Mesthrie 2012a:498). A parallel example from IE is *These mistakes may please be corrected* (Bhatt 2004:1022), showing *may* as a polite form for 'should'.

South African Indian English

South African Indian English is an interesting intermediary insofar as it is to some extent historically an offshoot of IE, while also to some extent starting afresh in plantations, cities and classrooms rooted in South Africa. Among the early influences on the growth of a distinct variety of English are: (a) the influence of Christian missionaries in Natal; (b) the influences of teachers, interpreters and clerks from India; (c) the expansion of education via schools begun by Indians and taken over as state-aided schools; and (d) influences from contact with Zulu and Afrikaans (Mesthrie 1992:18–22). SAIE might therefore be expected to share second language influences with its IE matrilect and its sister dialect of BSAE. Of the illustrative features cited above, all occur in SAIE's more basilectal and mesolectal varieties – see Mesthrie (2012b:507–10) for all citations below. Thus SAIE shows the use of non-count as count nouns: *staffs, furnitures*. It shows extension of the progressive to habitual and stative contexts, for example *She's working at Foschini's* (where the habitual verb form corresponds to standard English *She works at Foschini's*). SAIE shows the use of double conjunctions across clauses, for example *Though I visit Durban very often, but I don't like it*. As far as reduplication and pronouns are concerned, SAIE falls on the side of IE rather than BSAE: forms like *hot-hot samosas* are common, and the use of pronoun forms like *you-all* or *y'all*, with its genitive form *yall's* ('your pl.'). The *Dictionary of South African Indian English* (Mesthrie 2010b) gives a comprehensive overview of the diversity of sources for the vocabulary of this social dialect. There are retentions showing the influence of early teachers from India: *tuition(s)* ('special lessons outside class for which one pays a tutor'), *by-heart* ('to learn off by heart'), *alphabets* ('letters of the alphabet') and *further studies* ('higher education, tertiary studies'). From Zulu come terms for fruit like *madoni* (Zulu *indoni*, pl. *amadoni* 'forest myrtle') and *mutton-gulla* (Zulu *itungulu*, pl. *amatungulu* 'Natal plum'). Structurally, SAIE would appear to have much in common with its Indian matrilect. However, equally important is its subsequent co-existence with other varieties of English in South Africa, and its hierarchical relation with the historically dominant form of White L1 South African English (itself influenced by co-existence with Afrikaans and Afrikaans-influenced English). In this way SAIE has acquired a few forms that are unknown in IE: for example *and them* as associative plural marker (feature 52) as in *Roy-and-them came*. Conversely, there are two regular features of IE that are uncommon in SAIE. The first of these is the 'X is there' construction for standard English 'There is X' (feature 73). Thus, where standard English has *There's food*, IE has *Food is there*. This is largely unknown in SAIE, apart from a lone example in my corpus of 1992. Sharma (2012:527) supplies the related example *Son is there* for standard English 'I have a son'. The second difference is that plural form *-all* is attached to *you* in SAIE (as in IE), but not to other forms like *who-all* (feature 39).[5] Sharma supplies other IE forms unknown in SAIE: *they-all, them-all* and *we-all*. However, the form *that-all* for 'those kinds of things' is found among basilectal speakers of SAIE. Both IE and SAIE have the distributive reduplicated interrogative form *who-who* ('who of several people, who of disparate groups'), not reported elsewhere in South Africa. It would be interesting to monitor whether the large number of post-apartheid immigrants from South Asia will lead to the introduction (or reintroduction) of salient forms into SAIE like *who-all* and 'X is there'. My (corrigible) expectation is that it won't, and that the direction of diffusion of features will be from SAIE to the English of new migrants from India.

SAIE differs from traditional IE and BSAE in that it has become a first language for a majority of its speakers. In this process speakers have developed a vast stylistic range in which sub-varieties co-exist that are on one hand close to standard and on the other retain a large number of forms associated with the earlier process of second language acquisition. There is accordingly for many – but not all – speakers a dichotomy between an interactive and community-oriented style versus a more public and formal style. Thus whereas IE has been characterised as bureaucratic in style (Krishnaswamy & Burde 1998:89), or bookish with a 'moralistic tone' (Kachru 1983:39), SAIE shows the converse – hyper-colloquial forms except in the most formal contexts (Mesthrie 1992:22). A newer ingredient to this variety is the complexity introduced by post-apartheid schooling practices. It is now fairly common for young middle-class speakers of black, coloured and Indian backgrounds to show varying degrees of crossover patterns into speech that was once associated with whiteness. Amongst Indian youth this range covers four types: (a) a complete crossover (with jettisoning of SAIE norms);

(b) an intermediate variety that comprises SAIE with phonetic influences from White SAE; (c) a modified crossover variety that retains some traces of SAIE; and (d) bidialectalism with a 'white' crossover form used in certain social networks and an identifiable SAIE form used with family and certain Indian friends.

The Neighbor-Net Comparisons

Figure 1 is an update of a 'Neighbor-Net' diagram compiled by Kortmann and Lunkenheimer (2012:930), taking into account all 135 features of the 74 varieties originally studied in the project. In addition I include a 75th variety of interest to South Africa, namely Cape Flats English (i.e. the English of coloured people in Cape Town), based on research in progress. Neighbor-Net is a powerful statistical tool that arises out of bioinformatics and genetic modelling (Bryant & Moulton 2004) and has found favour in linguistic typological characterisations (Cysouw 2007). In figure 1 the different branches (or clusters) of the 'fallen tree' represent distinct subsets within the data arrived at on the basis of similarities in linguistic features, rather than by geographical location. A glance at the main branches will nevertheless show a large degree of geographical cohesion. The authors are at pains to stress that variety type (L1, L2, Pidgin or Creole) is an even stronger correlate than geography. As far as the present comparison is concerned, cluster 1,

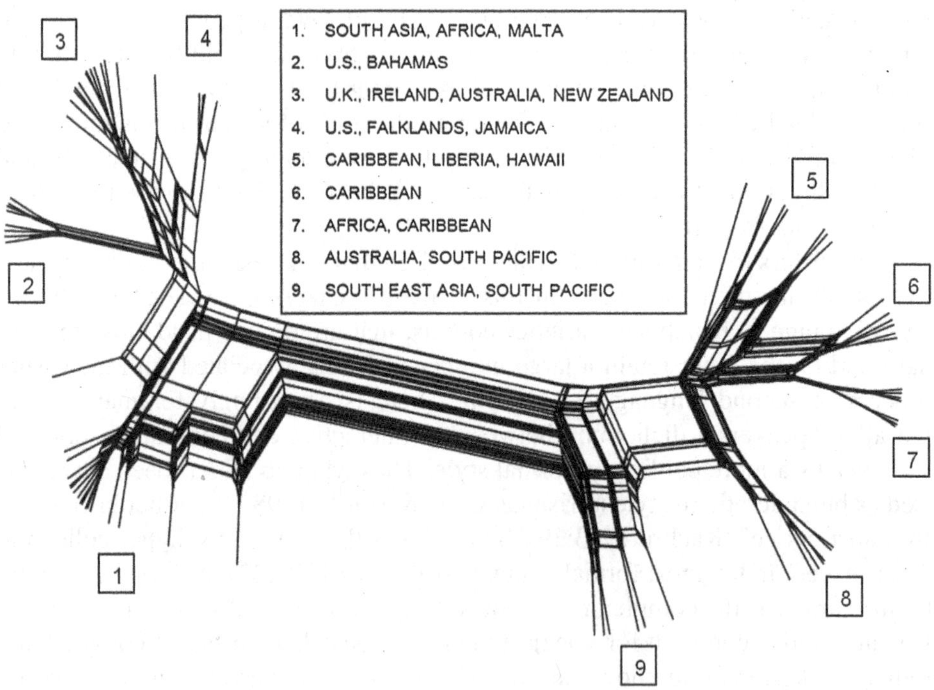

Figure 1. A Neighbor-Net comparison of 75 varieties of 'World Englishes', showing similarities in a set of 134 linguistic features (courtesy Kortmann & Lunkenheimer).

comprising South Asia, Africa and Malta, is of especial relevance. Cluster 7 comprises the Pidgin and Creole varieties of West Africa, while Butler English – a rudimentary pidgin of India – falls into cluster 9. Figure 2 provides a close-up of cluster 1, which is made up of varieties from disparate locations: chiefly Africa and South Asia (Sri Lanka, Pakistan, India); and isolated varieties from the South Pacific (Fiji); Southeast Asia (Philippines); and Europe (Malta). Africa presents the largest numbers of varieties in cluster 1: traditional L2 varieties of East Africa (Tanzania, Uganda, Kenya); West Africa (Ghana, Nigeria); Central Africa (Cameroon); the L1 varieties of whites in Zimbabwe and South Africa; and the remaining varieties of South Africa (black, coloured and Indian). Figure 2 shows the especially close structural relationships between the three varieties surveyed in this article: the L2 varieties of India and South Africa's black communities are adjacent, with the proviso that South African Indian English comes halfway between the two.

It needs to be stressed that Kortmann and Lunkenheimer's survey is a structural / typological one, and that the results might be different if one turns to other facets of language, for example phonetics, discourse structure, semantic and pragmatic features. Nevertheless, figure 2 speaks volumes of the similarities between the processes of second language (classroom) acquisition in colonial British contexts in

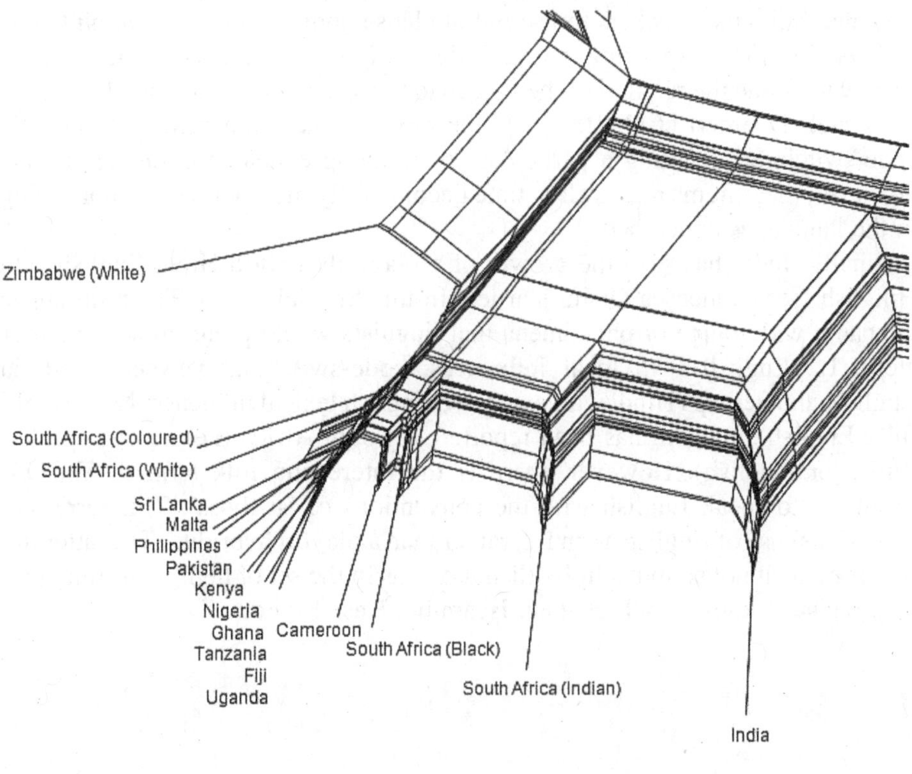

Figure 2. A close-up of the bottom left corner of figure 1, showing similarities between selected varieties in Africa and Asia, and Fiji and Malta (courtesy Kortmann & Lunkenheimer).

South Asia and Africa. It also suggests that the give-and-take of co-existence for two centuries make the L1 variety of White South African English a distinctly African affiliate rather than being in cluster 3 with the UK, Australia and New Zealand.

Conclusion: L2s, Linguistic Convergence and Hybridity

A focus on English in postcolonies without due regard to its multilingual context is not desirable. In all ESL countries there is ongoing convergence between English and the major indigenous languages. Kachru described this process as the Indianization of English and the Englishization of Hindi. (A better term for the latter might be 'Anglification'.) The former process has been outlined above. As far as the latter is concerned, Kachru (1983:204–5) cited the following new developments in Hindi: (a) use of indirect speech; (b) use of impersonal constructions; (c) use of passives with overtly stated agents; (d) increase in subject-verb-object sentences; and (e) use of parenthetical clauses. For major South African languages like Zulu and Xhosa something similar is noticeable, though one has to acknowledge the additional influence of Afrikaans. English structure has influenced Zulu and Xhosa in the number system, resulting in a co-existence of the indigenous system with base 5 and the decimal system of English. Equally striking is the frequent use of logical connectors and discourse markers from English. It is a mark of educated bilingual speakers to use initial clause conjunctions like *so, and, but, if* and *because*, while speaking Xhosa, Zulu etc. Discourse markers which function largely to define the relation of the speech to the speaker are also notable: *I mean, I think* etc. (Deumert et al. 2006). At the moment these are better considered as code-switching, denoting a particular style among educated bilingual speakers. However, these items may well in time become fully incorporated (as borrowings) in the languages concerned.

Finally, India has seen the growth of a playfully hybrid Hindi-English called Hinglish (see Francesca Orsini's article in this Special Issue). The term appears to span a wide range of phenomena that linguists would prefer to analyse separately: L2 English with local influences, code-switching between Hindi and English, and perhaps Hindi with extensive English lexical influence. No such playfully English amalgam has been reported in South Africa (i.e. no one speaks of Zulish or Xholish). However, there is the interesting folk term *to Xhosalise*, meaning 'to speak English with the conventions of isiXhosa'. This term refers to 'serious' use of English as an L2, rather than a playful hybridity. The latter function is evident not so much in English usage as in the set of highly informal township registers known as Tsotsitaal, Iscamtho, Kasi Taal etc.

Notes

1. L2 or 'second language' is often a linguistic cover term for a chronological second, third, fourth etc language, seen from the viewpoint of an individual's acquisition of language.
2. 16 June 1920.
3. The categories used by the editors were slightly different, but do not affect the present analysis: low-contact traditional L1 dialects; high-contact L1 varieties; L2 varieties; Pidgins; Creoles.
4. Several influences converge to provide this effect: Afrikaans, English, Indian languages and possibly Indonesian languages.
5. *Who-all* is reported as a frequent form in White South African English (Bowerman 2012). Intriguingly, while the form occurs in this variety and IE, it is noticeably absent in SAIE.

References

Agnihotri, R.K. & Singh, R. (eds). 2012. *Indian English: Towards a New Paradigm.* Noida, India: Orient Blackswan.

Alexander, N. 1989. *Language Policy and National Unity in South Africa/Azania.* Cape Town: Buchu Books.

Badassy, P. 2002. 'Turbans and Top Hats: Indian Interpreters in the Colony of Natal: 1880–1910'. Unpublished Honours thesis, University of Natal.

Bhatt, R. 2004. 'Indian English: Syntax', in B. Kortmann, E.W. Schneider, K. Burridge, R. Mesthrie & C. Upton (eds), *A Handbook of Varieties of English, Vol. 2. Morphology and Syntax.* Berlin: Mouton de Gruyter.

Bowerman, S. 2012. 'White South African English', in Kortmann & Lunkenhimer (eds), *The Mouton World Atlas of Variation in English.* Berlin: Mouton de Gruyter.

Brain, J.B. 1983. *Christian Indians in Natal.* Cape Town: Oxford University Press.

Bryant, D. & Moulton, V. 2004. 'Neighbor-Net: An Agglomerative Method for the Construction of Phylogenetic Networks'. *Molecular Biology and Evolution* 21(2):255–65.

Chomsky, N. 1965. *Aspects of the Theory of Syntax.* Cambridge, MA: MIT Press.

Cysouw, M. 2007. 'New Approaches to Cluster Analysis of Typological Indices', in R. Köhler & P. Grzbek (eds), *Exact Methods in the Study of Language and Text.* Berlin/New York: Mouton de Gruyter.

Deumert, A., Hurst, E., Masinyana, O. & Mesthrie, R. 2006. 'Logical Connectors and Discourse Markers in Urban IsiXhosa'. Paper presented at the Linguistics Society of Southern Africa conference, University of KwaZulu-Natal.

Hardgrave, R.L. 1965. 'The Riots in Tamilnad: Problems and Prospects of India's Language Crisis'. *Asian Survey* (8):399–407.

Kachru, B.B. 1983. *The Indianization of English.* New Delhi: Oxford University Press.

Kachru, B.B. 1988. 'The Sacred Cows of English'. *English Today* 16:3–8.

Kortmann, B. & Lunkenheimer, K. (eds). 2012. *The Mouton World Atlas of Variation in English.* Berlin: De Gruyter Mouton.

Krishnaswani, N. & Burde, A. 1998. *The Politics of Indians' English: Linguistic Colonialism and the Expanding English Empire.* New Delhi: Oxford University Press.

Lange, C. 2012. *The Syntax of Spoken Indian English.* Amsterdam: Benjamins.

Mair, C. 2003. 'Kreolismen und verbales Identitätsmanagement im geschrieben Jamaikanischen English', in E. Vogel, A. Napp & W. Lutterer (eds), *Zwischen Ausgrenzung und Hybridisierung.* Würzburg: Ergon.

Makalela, L. 2004. 'Making Sense of BSAE for Linguistic Democracy in South Africa'. *World Englishes* 23(3):355–66 <DOI 10.1111/j.0883-2919>.

McKinney, C. 2013. 'Orientations to English in Post-apartheid Schooling'. *English Today* 29(1):22–7.

Mehrotra, R.R. 1998. *Indian English: Tests and Interpretations.* Amsterdam: Benjamins.

Mesthrie, R. 1989. 'The Origins of Fanagalo'. *Journal of Pidgin and Creole Languages* 4(2):211–40.

Mesthrie, R. 1992. *English in Language Shift: The History, Structure and Sociolinguistics of South African Indian English.* Cambridge: Cambridge University Press.

Mesthrie, R. 1993. 'Gandhi and Language Politics'. *Bua* 8(4):4–7.

Mesthrie, R. 2002. 'Language Change, Survival, Decline: Indian Languages in South Africa', in R. Mesthrie (ed), *Language in South Africa*. Cambridge: Cambridge University Press.

Mesthrie, R. 2010a. 'Socio-phonetics and Social Change: Deracialisation of the GOOSE Vowel in South African English'. *Journal of Sociolinguistics* 14(1):3–33.

Mesthrie, R. 2010b. *A Dictionary of South African Indian English*. Cape Town: UCT Press.

Mesthrie, R. 2012a. 'Black South African English', in Kortmann & Lunkenhimer (eds), *The Mouton World Atlas of Variation in English*. Berlin: Mouton de Gruyter.

Mesthrie, R. 2012b. 'Indian South African English', in Kortmann & Lunkenhimer (eds), *The Mouton World Atlas of Variation in English*. Berlin: Mouton de Gruyter.

Metcalf, B.D. & Metcalf, T.R. 2006. *A Concise History of Modern India*. Cambridge: Cambridge University Press.

Mufwene, S. 2001. *The Ecology of Language Evolution*. Cambridge: Cambridge University Press.

Nihalani, P., Tongue, R.K., Hosali, P. & Crowther, J. 2004. *Indian and British English: A Handbook of Usage and Pronunciation* 2nd edition. New Delhi: Oxford University Press.

Paulasto, H. 2014. 'Extended Uses of the Progressive Form in L1 and L2 Englishes'. *English World Wide* 35(3):247–76 <DOI 10.1075/eww.35.3.01pau>.

Schneider, E. 2003 'The Dynamics of New Englishes: From Identity Construction to Dialect Birth'. *Language* 79(2):233–81.

Schneider, E. 2007. *Postcolonial English: Varieties around the World*. Cambridge: Cambridge University Press.

Sedlatschek, A. 2009. *Contemporary Indian English – Variation and Change*. Amsterdam: Benjamins.

Sharma, D. 2009. 'Typological Diversity in New Englishes'. *English World Wide* 30(2):170–95.

Sharma, D. 2012. 'Indian English', in Kortmann & Lunkenhimer (eds), *The Mouton World Atlas of Variation in English*. Berlin: Mouton de Gruyter.

Sinha, S.P. 1978. *English in India: A Historical Study with Particular Reference to English Education in India*. Patna: Janaki Prakashan.

Toefy, T. 2014. 'Sociophonetics and Class Differentiation: A Study of Working- and Middle-class English in Cape Town's Coloured Community'. Unpublished PhD thesis, University of Cape Town.

Van Rooy, B. 2006. 'The Extension of the Progressive Aspect in Black South African English'. *World Englishes* 25(1):37–64 <DOI 10.1111/j.0083-2919>.

Van Rooy, B. 2014. 'Progressive Aspect and Stative Verbs in Outer Circle Varieties'. *World Englishes* 33(2):157–72 <DOI 10.1111/weng.12079>.

Wilmot, K. 2014. '"Coconuts" and the Middle Class: Identity Change and the Emergence of a New Prestigious English Variety in South Africa'. *English World-Wide* 35(3):306–37 <DOI 10. 1075/eww.35.3.03wil>.

Dil Maange More: Cultural Contexts of Hinglish in Contemporary India

Francesca Orsini

University of London

After over a century of language nationalism and almost as long a period of intense competition and mutual contempt, in post-liberalisation and post-low caste assertion India the boundaries between English and Hindi have recently become more porous, and the hold of both 'pure Hindi' and 'British/pure English' has become much more limited. English is of course still the language of greater opportunities in local and global terms, and increasingly so, but as low-caste politicisation and literacy widen the sphere of Hindi, and the 'new middle class' remains resolutely bilingual in its everyday and entertainment practices, the relation between English and Hindi has become more a relationship of parallel expansion, though still perceived in public discourse as a zero-sum game.

> A vivacious mixture of English and native tongues, Hinglish is a dialect pulsating with energy and invention that captures the essential fluidity of Indian society. (Deep Kanta Datta-Ray, quoted in Jaikrishan 2011)

> It's a bridge between two cultures that has become an island of its own, a distinct hybrid culture for people who aspire to make it rich abroad without sacrificing the sassiness of the mother tongue. And it may soon claim more native speakers worldwide than English. (Baldauf 2004)

> The real triumph of the rise of Hinglish isn't that it's beaten back the English of, well, the English. That brand of English doesn't exist any more; in India, it's under siege from students who're rattoing too hard for their papers, yaar, to care whether they're speaking the Queen's English or some joshed-up masala mix. (Roy 2004)

> It's India's self-confident voice rising above the subservience that was once expressed in an English way . . . 'Hinglish' is all about the ascendant and emergent force that is modern India. If language reflects national identity, the speed at which 'Hinglish' is being adopted sends out very loud cultural and economic signals to the rest of the world. (Khanna 2010)

These are some of the upbeat claims that are being made on behalf of Hinglish, a moniker used to cover a wide range of code-switching and mixed language phenomena that combine English and Hindi.[1] In common parlance in India Hinglish indexes code-switching and language mixing between English and Hindi within either an English or Hindi matrix, but also Indian English as well as English in Devanagari script or Hindi in Roman script.[2] But while from a linguistic point of view Hindi cannot be considered a stabilised Creole or a fused lect, the fact that a single term is used for what several commentators have pointed out are a multitude of different varieties, practices, registers, styles, trends, and social forces is itself significant, since one of the large claims being made for Hinglish is that it is a unifying force that is breaking down once stiff social barriers between English and Hindi (or EMT and HMT).[3] As such, Hinglish is presented not just as the language of urban/metropolitan youth culture, but also as the language of a new, enterprising and confident India, in which skills and the right attitude trump social and caste background, and economic prosperity and global presence have translated into a growing confidence in one's own culture and language.[4] Hinglish is projected as *both* the informal language of the globalised Indian middle class *and* the aspirational language of the upwardly-mobile vernacular lower-middle, middle, and working classes who are 'asking for more', but who clearly have very different linguistic repertoires and grasp of and within the two languages.

Code-mixing and switching between English and Hindi (and other Indian languages) has a long history that goes back to colonial times, and Hindi, like other Indian languages, has an equally long history of accommodating English loanwords (Snell 1990; Sharma 2011). Mixing was then largely a phenomenon of spoken language, though some, but by no means all, writers also used it in writing, usually for satirical purposes or in order to valorise linguistic inventiveness and current language practices.[5] By comparison, what we see from the 1990s onwards, i.e. in the post-liberalisation period, is a new tolerance, indeed a *preference* for Hinglish in the various guises mentioned above in a host of contexts where mixing would not have been allowed or was a marginal phenomenon before: TV news, newspapers, advertising, Hindi film dialogues and songs, etc. Indeed, the 26 September 2011 government circular that directed civil servants and clerks to write their files in 'simple Hindi', i.e. Hindi with current English words rather than Sanskrit coinages, aroused public controversy but also showed that an official barrier had been pulled down.[6]

As an example of code-mixing and code-switching, Hinglish has been studied extensively by linguists, who typically focus on live spoken interactions between individuals.[7] A few linguists have studied language mixing in *scripted* cultural products such as TV serials, films, and novels, and their approaches provide valuable models for textual and cultural studies scholars.[8] But while linguists have been meticulous in tracking and analysing speakers' interactions, when it comes to the broader cultural and social fields in which these interactions take place and the meanings they carry, their categories can become quite generic. For this reason, it seemed useful to disarticulate Hinglish and try and identify the specific contexts in which speakers as well as cultural products use Hinglish as sub-fields, each with its own institutions, forces, and logics, and where different language ideologies coexist or clash.[9] Moreover, the intense re-mixing, re-use, and re-accenting of Hinglish catchphrases such as '*Dil Maange More*' (this heart asks for/longs for more) or 'Emotional *atyachaar*' (emotional torture) show how much Hinglish is a consciously citational code (with invisible inverted commas), constructed and circulated through the commercial systems of advertising, TV media, films, and radio, which in turn eagerly pick up innovative phrases from speakers.[10] In this perspective, even the historical tendency to include English loanwords can become a self-conscious, re-accented, usage.[11] By surveying advertising, news media and politics, the workplace, education and college life, films, film songs and TV reality shows, this article begins to disaggregate the varying contexts in which what is generally called Hinglish works. As such, it offers a research agenda and research context rather than specific case studies. Hinglish as a trend attracts intense public and media interest, and as a consequence this article relies heavily on public commentary through newspapers and blogs.

Language Ideologies

Debates around Hinglish in public media refract the polarisation between the ideology of Hindi as 'mother tongue', 'national language' and 'the language of the people', which comes wrapped up with national pride, echoes of the anti-colonial struggle, and class critiques of English privilege, and the ideology of English as the language of opportunities and of social and spatial mobility (LaDousa 2014). So entrenched have these positions become in almost 70 years of India's independence that different opinions, for example those recommending English-Hindi bilingualism, get automatically slotted into one of the two positions, either English-*wala* or Hindi-*wala*.[12] 'Hindi views' on Hinglish, as in the case of the 2011 government circular, tend to frown at it as a conspiracy by the English-*walas* that ought to be stopped and strenuously resisted (Dube 2014). Even to study it with interest, or to view it as a social and cultural phenomenon that individuals can hardly stop, amounts to collusion according to this view. Popular English writing on Indian English for a long time looked down on Indian English, language mixing, and Indian influences on English with a mixture of disapproval, humour and forced acceptance (for example John 2007). But as already mentioned above, Indian English/Hinglish is now viewed more enthusiastically as capturing the current, post-liberalisation Zeitgeist:

> When Zee began airing a daily Hinglish news bulletin almost 18 years to the date, it seemed like a bad joke. Nowadays, however, Hinglish is widely accepted as the lingua franca of the young, allowing advertisers and producers of TV reality shows to overcome language barriers and reach out to a pan-Indian audience . . .
>
> Indians have this remarkable ability to shuttle between idioms, as if they were two neighbouring balconies, joined by an invisible passage. The music of *Delhi Belly* moves from KL Saigal to punk, just like Indian girls today manage to slip out of a short black dress and into a sari with startling ease and self-confidence. (Mehrotra n.d.)

And if the dominant post-liberalisation discourse has partly been about the struggle of the new India to 'free' itself from the old fettles, it is clear which side Hinglish is perceived to be on:

> There are two Indias in this country. One India is straining at the leash, eager to spring forward and live up to all the adjectives that the world has increasingly been showering upon us. The other India is the leash. One India says, 'Give me a chance and I'll prove myself'. The other India says, 'Prove yourself first and maybe then you'll have a choice'. One India lives in the optimism of our hearts. The other lurks in the skepticism of our minds ... (*Times of India* TV commercial, in O'Barr 2008)

From this perspective, critiques of English privilege are often received as critiques of social mobility.

Yet rather than simply aligned with English in the Hindi-English debate, we can also view Hinglish as championing bilingualism and the ability to recognise and move between linguistic codes. The heroine of Anuja Chauhan's chick-lit novel *The Zoya Factor* (2008:207) wonders about mono-linguals as she enters Australia, 'People who knew only one language ... which was *weird*. Because, hello, what would they switch to if they started getting pally, or angry, or fell in love?' If Hinglish, in Santosh Desai's words, 'allows us, in some ways, to loosen the idea of English, especially around the margins' and opens up 'the boundaries that generally separate English from other languages', at the same time it has also helped Hindi to acquire a brand (cool *desi*), using a visual language that circulates in music videos, advertising, and photography (Desai 2010:201).[13]

Yet how inclusive is Hinglish? And is it one phenomenon or is it many, whose meanings and dynamics vary from domain to domain – from news media, politics, education, and work to advertising, films, music, youth culture and so on? If one of the reasons given for the success of Hinglish is that it allows communication and breaks down barriers, its different realisations bear traces of the social group to which the speaker belongs, and thus Hinglish still subtly indexes class stratification through accent, inflection, word choice, etc. As Devyani Sharma points out, this makes Hinglish a paradox:

> If you use fluent Hinglish, particularly mixing standard urban Hindi and English that you have been exposed to, it may be seen as a metropolitan privilege. In other kinds of Hinglish, there are indications of reduced competence and aspirations of upward mobility. (2011:205)

The crucial question, as she puts it, 'is not only that of the speaker but the one receiving it, hearing it, and *locating the speaker in a particular class*. This will always make Hinglish a part of a stratified context and it *cannot* become, in totality, a unifying force' (Sharma 2011, my emphasis). For this reason, for each example and domain in this article I will raise questions of inclusion and stratification. While I am mindful of linguists' warnings about the danger of imputing meanings to the codes speakers use,[14] I will still do so when interpreting cultural products and performances, because their self-conscious use and mixing of different registers and accents of Hindi and English, word and phrase creativity, and implicit or explicit reference to language ideologies of English and Hindi make strong appeals to group identity (whether existing or imagined) and cultural and social distinction.

Yeh Dil Maange More

Advertising has rightly been seen as crucial to the transformations of post-liberalisation India, facilitating the penetration of multi-national corporations (MNC) products and as a laboratory for manufacturing the 'new middle class' dreams of affluent lifestyles and its aspiration of being both global and rooted in India. Advertising, Harish Trivedi notes, is also the one domain where Hinglish is now not the exception but the rule (Kothari & Snell 2011:xviii). Simply translating MNC English slogans into Hindi, one advertising executive says, did not work: 'You may be understood, *but not vibed with*. That's why all the multi-national corporations in India now speak Hinglish in their ads.'[15] Thus Pantene's 'Come on girls, it's your time to shine' became 'Come on girls, *waqt hai shine karne ka!*' Thanks to former JTW India vice-president and executive creative director-turned novelist Anuja Chauhan, Pepsi's 'Ask for more' became '*Yeh Dil Maange More*' (This heart asks/longs for more), with its clever alliteration between *Maange* and *More* and use of the subjunctive and of an elongated *aa* to visually and phonetically express longing.[16] Chauhan pioneered Hinglish in advertising with catch-lines for Pepsi like the impatient question '*Mera Number Kab Aayega*' (When will my number/turn come?), the bubbly Punjabiesque '*Oye Bubbly*', as well as '*KitKat Break Banta Hai*' (KitKat means/needs a break).[17] One of the many ads with *Mera Number Kab Aayega* features first a little boy in a playground awaiting his turn at the swings, then a boy overlooked by the basketball coach, and finally a boy who wants to kiss a girl: every time the boy asks, 'When is my turn going to come?' In the last scene, first the voice-over says, '*Ab to aa hi jaayega*' (Now it *will* come), because Pepsi bottle crowns then carried lucky numbers that led to big prizes, and then the boy, assured, repeats, '*Mera number aayega*' (My turn *will* come). In the words of an advertising professional:

> It's a funny ad because, first, [the boy] looks like the perfect loser, and secondly, because, even at the end of the ad, he is a loser. His number still hasn't come. No brand wanted to associate with a loser. But with this ad, we tried to connect, not with the winner, but with the millions who wouldn't win. (Quoted in Khanna 2010)

In advertising the linguistic inventiveness and creativity of Hinglish is exploited as a shortcut to 'intimacy', the keyword JWT executive Swati Bhattacharya used with me.[18] It also carries meanings of rootedness for the English-educated and of social mobility (and of course dreams and aspirations) for the 'vernacular' masses.

Hinglish in advertising consists of either a Hindi or mixed-language catch-line in Roman script or an English catch-line in Devanagari script, and language switches and/or mixes between the visual slogan and brand name, the characters' dialogues or monologues, the jingle's song, and the catch-line spoken by the character or the voice-over. Switches may also include shifts in accent and register (Indian English vs international English, regional variety vs formal Hindi), and intertexual references to film dialogues or songs. Each mix or shift, whether of code or script, unsettles the steadiness of the language in order to create an informal, intimate connection with the viewer. A connection that advertisers seek to transform into a steady relationship and brand loyalty over a series of storied ads.

Two of the many ads for the Pepsi '*Yeh Dil Maange More*' campaign help us see the range of cultural idioms that just one campaign draws upon, and how the ads interpret the idea of aspiration (This heart longs for more) for different target audiences. In the first ad, an 'ordinary' and bored Mumbai college student is dazzled by a nightly vision of Bollywood stars Rani Mukherjee, Shahrukh Khan and Kajol, which turns into a personal encounter when they dance for and with him. The song says 'Live more, ask for more' (*Jiyo more, maango more*).[19] In another ad from the same campaign we see village children dreaming of their cricket hero Sachin Tendulkar (cricket of course being one of the dream avenues of socio-economic mobility) while a rusty bicycle brings a rusty container of Pepsi bottles – 'backward' village India as seen through a beautiful patina of warm and vibrant colours. The song, a catchy tune in the rough voice of a folk singer on a single-stringed instrument, reads the Hindi word *pyas* as thirst for a drink but also for a better life, unfettered and unshackled:

> *Aihe, ghumar-ghumarkar! ghumar ghumarkar jiya garje, dil yah bole, jhumke bole, tare jhume, pyaas bari hai aur bhi barh le use, kholke bandhan, torke taale yeh dil maange more*!
>
> [Oho, round and round, round and round roars the heart, speaks the heart, swings the heart, soar the stars, says the heart – I'm so thirsty! Thirst even more, free the latches, break the locks, this heart longs for more!][20]

Although both ads are technically all in Hindi, the Hinglish catch-line is enough to convey the Hinglish 'vibe'.

At the same time, while projecting aspirational lifestyles ad agencies of course are intensely conscious of and work with precise target groups defined in terms of age, gender, economic power *and* language (EMT vs VMT/HMT or Vernacular- or Hindi-Medium Types being widespread acronyms), thus reproducing hierarchies and differences that they are ostensibly also removing. Zoya, the heroine and advertising executive in the novel *The Zoya Factor,* looks down at Junior Maximilk ads which target 'Socio-Economic Category B+ (education: graduation, family income: 30,000 per month or less, language of choice: Hindi)' (Chauhan 2008:116). Even a sympathetic professional like Santosh Desai, MD and CEO of Futurebrands India Ltd., who believes that 'Advertising can play a powerful role if it creates a ladder of aspirations that inspires consumers to continuously move up in their lives,' points out that lower-income groups are either absent or caricatured:

> When was the last time you saw a village in a commercial that was not out of a tourist brochure? Barring a few instances, advertising excludes large parts of India from its mental model of consumers. This is particularly true for rural India but also applies to a whole set of mass-market consumers at the lower end.

> When it does depict them, it is most often as caricatures for the amusement of the rest of us. The implicit perspective is so metro oriented that Lucknow is seen as a small town and spoken down to. The 'us versus them' mindset is embedded deeply and conversations with 'people like them' are usually patronising, stereotypical or both. (Desai 2010)

In this, he views advertising as 'part of a larger discourse that includes popular cinema and news media where the rich have become the centre of our universe' (Desai 2010) and where the definition of 'ordinary people' in public discourse, at least in English, has sharply moved upwards.[21] While advertising, and the role of Hinglish in it, embodies the dominant discourse of post-liberalisation middle-class aspirations, mobility, and self-confidence, other domains display quite different dynamics and question triumphalistic narratives of mobility and inclusion.

News Media and Politics

While the 'traditional' hierarchy of English and Hindi journalism has not disappeared in terms of social, cultural and economic capital (particularly visible where groups own both English and Hindi newspapers), the great boom in Hindi news media that Robin Jeffrey (2000) has called 'newspaper revolution' and that includes also TV news channels such as NDTV and Aaj Tak has turned Hindi into the bigger player (see also Ninan 2007).[22] In the film *Peepli: Live!* (2010), Hindi journalist Deepak says: 'Who watches [English news]? We are the true journalists, who feel the pulse of the people (*janta*).'

This Hindi media boom has had repercussions on language policy in the media. While Hindi newspapers were successful in the past in popularising Sanskritic neologisms, more recently they have debated whether to accept Hinglish and allow current English words (in Devanagari script). This is particularly true of *Navbharat Times,* the Hindi paper of the *Times of India* group. As *Times of India* Rahul Kansal says, 'Our Hindi editors are told to use as many English words as the readers are used to – and it helps' (in Kothari & Snell 2011:206).[23] The pure Hindi of Doordarshan news, the Indian state TV, which was equally feared and made fun of in the past as impenetrable to all but the Hindi highly-educated, is a thing of the past even on that channel. Part of the 'newspaper revolution' has been the growth of tabloid news supplements with an intense coverage of Bollywood and TV celebrities which have imported the older popular film gossip mode of address that pioneered Hinglish (Parameswaran 2012:15). There have also been experiments such as the Hinglish newspaper *I-next,* which is basically in Hindi but has many English headings in Devanagari script.

This Hindi newspaper and news channel revolution must be seen in connection with the rise of regional parties and of low-caste politicisation. This creates an interesting tension: while TV news channels can be accused of providing a strongly metro-centric perspective on news – the central theme of Anusha Rizvi's film *Peepli: Live!*, along the lines of Santosh Desai's critique quoted above – Hindi newspapers and local cable TV news channels such as Citi

Hulchul in Meerut have focused strongly on local and regional news. So while small-town and village India in Hindi films or advertisements appear mainly as a backdrop, which cool kids who speak the metropolitan youth lingo of Hinglish escape from, local news actors (and politicians) speak a different Hinglish, with a Hindi matrix despite the abundance of English words.

Linguistic and rhetorical skills are of course crucial to politics, and the ability to speak Hindi (or other regional languages) has been a must for politicians in north India ever since the rise of electoral politics in the 1920s, though Hindi-only proficiency becomes a handicap at the national level. This is a topic that requires much more systematic research, but we can begin by observing that at a basic level Hinglish code-switching and language mixing have become a mainstay of political discourse in north India,[24] yet if we pay attention to *accent, fluency, and rhetorical skills*, very different types of Hinglish and bilingualism emerge, not just due to a politician's background and education, but also aimed at sending out particular signals to voters.

Thus in the 2012 elections in the Hindi-speaking state of Uttar Pradesh two 'young' leaders were pitted against each other in the polls. Rahul Gandhi, clearly metropolitan and more comfortable with English, made a big but ultimately unsuccessful effort at appearing rooted and committed to the local constituency, and speaking in correct Hindi was part of this effort. But as his speech in Phulpur shows, his competence in Hindi did not amount to rhetorical competence.[25] By contrast, the winner Akhilesh Yadav, first-generation English (and Australia-) educated, who speaks English with a strong accent, was careful to project the image of a Hindi politician; while at ease in the world of English and of technology, he was keen to downplay his English and foreign education, and commentators judged that his perceived rootedness (also expressed in his Hindi rhetorical ease) contributed significantly to his victory.[26] And when former UP chief minister and Dalit leader Mayawati, who has always projected herself as a representative of the lower-caste (Dalit-Bahujan) masses and has always spoken in Hindi with a strong local accent, strained to include a large number of English words in an interview, it was to strengthen her short-lived prime ministerial bid and to show that she was able to work at the national and international levels.[27]

Compared to other domains, then, in the post-liberalisation period news media and politics have seen the importance of Hindi and of regional roots *grow*, and it is an English accent, rather than a Hindi one, that is perceived as a hindrance. This trend has recently received a fillip from the prime minister, Narendra Modi, who instructed his ministers to speak in Hindi in public as much as possible; though as one commentator showed, in his speech from Delhi's Red Fort on Independence Day 2014, he spoke only in Hindi for the first ten minutes to emphasise his cultural identity, but then switched to Hinglish catch-phrases and slogans when he talked about his plans for economic development.[28] English TV news no longer dub or subtitle Hindi politicians' statements, and the same is true for Hindi TV news with statements in English, a clear indication of how expectations of viewers' understanding of and tolerance for the other language have changed.

At the same time, politics and news media are also where the Hindi vs English language debate periodically resurfaces, with well-rehearsed and valid arguments against English privilege and social exclusion or Hindi's fustiness and unfair imposition, and in favour of the expediency of English or the social inclusivity and reach of Hindi.[29]

Hinglish in the Workplace

In the world of the information technology (IT) boom and globalisation, English is of course pursued as the key to success for knowledge professionals and anyone aspiring to a good job (Upadhya & Vasavi 2008). This is one reason for the exponential growth of private English-*speaking* courses in small towns and metropolitan centres, not only to improve communicative skills but also to build self-confidence, alongside (and synonymous with?) courses in personality development.[30] Within this environment of intense investment in the English language as the key to professional success and social mobility even for groups who would not have dreamt of it a generation earlier, how does Hinglish play out? To what extent has the workplace become more inclusive and disregards accent or language repertoires?[31] Studying the presence and use of Hinglish at the workplace means paying attention not just to workers' practices in the workplace but also to the language dimensions of workers' management in the new economy.

In the English-speaking professional workplace of large companies, Hinglish seems to exist only to mark a level of informality.[32] At the lower end of the IT sector, language becomes part of worker's management. For BPO (i.e. call centre) jobs, language and accent coaching are a regular and substantial part of workers' training, given the very high turnover of workers.[33] So while the triumphalistic discourse of Hinglish that harnesses it to Indian English and projects it as a variety of English that will acquire the same international legitimacy as American English and British English, in BPOs Hinglish is seen as a barrier that needs to be overcome. There Hinglish and Hindi/Indian languages can only be 'furtive tongues' (Krishnamurthy 2011). But in the ITES workplace itself, among workers who are overwhelmingly young and who, according to AR Vasavi (in Upadhya & Vasavi 2008), like to distinguish themselves from other workers by their (higher) education qualifications and consumption habits, and redefine their work as education and entertainment, Hinglish seems to have a strong hold together with other aspects of metropolitan consumerist youth culture such as food or clothing.

At the same time, as scholars point out, one of the largest areas of employment growth – in India as elsewhere – has been at the lower end of the informal sector: maintenance, security, catering, cleaning ('housekeeping') etc.[34] While substantive research still needs to be carried out, informal enquiries suggest that basic English/Hinglish is very much part of the training and (monitored) performance of such jobs, together with appearance (uniform), manners and body comportment. And while Hinglish allows for communication between the vastly different classes of those who frequent shopping malls or gated-housing communities and those who guard them or clean them, it can hardly bridge the vast gap between the linguistic competence, economic and social power between them. Poor English/Hinglish is often taken by wealthy residents/consumers as a sign of poor intelligence and a sign that 'they' are not 'like us'.[35] Here Hinglish works less as a language of socio-economic mobility and more as one of servitude.

Education and College Life

Education is a crucial area *both* for aspirations of social mobility *and* for the reproduction of social division – roughly corresponding to the division between 'private' and 'government' schools and English- and Hindi-medium, though both kinds of schools comprise a great variety and stratification in terms of quality of education (LaDousa 2014). A direct inheritance of the colonial education system, in the two-tier system, educationist Krishna Kumar has often pointed out, Hindi-medium education is not seen as a separate project but as a 'cheap edition' of English education. Thanks to the colonial (and postcolonial) organisation of knowledge, knowledge flows from English into the vernaculars, with teachers and schoolchildren often complaining about the poor quality of textbooks badly translated from English. The result is that despite the basic similarity between the two kinds of education, the language division creates right from childhood people who live in two different worlds. These separate worlds metamorphose into class consciousness created by the particular environment, cultural symbols and practices of the schools and from the 'common knowledge' that surrounds them (Kumar 2001).[36] While the failure to invest in universal primary education can be counted as one of the great blunders of post-independence India, the last decade or so has seen both a renewed government effort at meeting targets for basic literacy and primary education in rural areas, and the remarkable growth in demand for English-medium private schools even among the poor (see for example Ramalingam 2009), thus decreasing the demand for government schools. Despite long-standing studies by Indian educationists on the advantages of first-language primary education in the child's learning process (including language-learning skills), there is very strong popular perception that in order to learn good English so as to join the enchanted circle of English-speakers and gain access to the opportunities they have, a child must learn English from the youngest age possible. In order to achieve that aim many schools enforce a rule that prohibits speaking in one's first language in the pre-school and primary school space so as to avoid first-language interference. Two direct consequences of the boom in private English-medium schools and of their insistence on English-only proficiency that devalues first-language skills are first, limited competence in English despite attending English-medium schools because of the poor quality of teaching and of the teachers' own proficiency; and second, decreasing *written* and *reading* competence in one's first language in English-medium schools, so much so that one can apply many of the observations on language shift in migrant communities to Indian schoolchildren within India (for studies on language shift, see

Auer 1998). As a result, the competence in reading and writing Hindi English-educated children becomes strictly functional.

Against this background of formal English enforcement and aspiration, Hinglish nonetheless plays a crucial role in education and school/college life, both as a 'furtive tongue' and a necessary bridge, and as an informal and inclusive language identity. Many college teachers testify to the pragmatic need to use a mixture of English and Hindi to teach students who ostensibly went through an English education, and to create their own teaching materials in the absence of Hindi translations of key texts.[37] College teachers are also among those raising concerns that the growth of Hinglish and of bilingual *spoken* competence may occur at the expense of developing a full vocabulary in either language, so that speakers cannot operate *without* mixing.[38]

At the same time, Hinglish has emerged as the informal language of choice of college students, at least in metropolitan centres, for whom Hinglish may have indeed acquired the status of a sociolect (Kidwai 2014). College students view Hinglish both as a unifying medium for those coming from different regional backgrounds with varying bilingual competence, and as giving them a group identity:

> 'Yes, its true that there is a certain divide between those who speak good English and those who do not. Most of the outstation students, for instance are not too comfortable with the language, and thus, feel left out. I think that is the very reason why the "Indianised" version of English has become so popular. It has helped to make things less formal, and to generally, make everyone feel accepted,' says Shreya Mukherjee.
>
> 'I believe that the reason why Hinglish is so popular is because of the fact that it's a very "young" language. It has a certain funk-factor. In our college, none of us speak in proper Hindi or English, its always Hinglish that we prefer, and why not? It's one of the most creative and flexible languages. We end up creating a new word everyday and its so much fun,' laughs off Ramandeep Singh, a student from Chandigarh. (Quoted in Chowdhury 2008)

The close connection between college life and Hinglish is evident in the number of Hinglish poems on the web that deal with college studies, in the Hinglish spoken by college students in TV reality shows such as Channel V's *Dare 2 Date*, and in the perception that the new kind of *hatke* films often set in Delhi (*Oye Lucky Lucky Oye, Delhi Belly*, etc) that have Hinglish dialogues and feature college-going metropolitan youth are 'realistic' and 'represent' both young people and the language they speak. As we have seen, the presence of Hinglish in the professional workplace is also viewed as a direct spillover of Hinglish as the language shared by college-educated youth, evoking the same mood of camaraderie and fun.

Films and Television

Together with advertising, Hindi cinema is one of the domains in which Hinglish code-switching and language mixing have become most visible in the last decade, notwithstanding the longer history of English in Hindi films (Kothari & Snell 2011). A vigorous debate is going on in film circles concerning the currency of

Hinglish and the new crop of films that embrace it, and the consequences of this turn for the economics of film exhibition and distribution. A parallel discourse concerns the aesthetics of Hinglish in film songs. In the context of cinema, Hinglish seems to indicate films that may be almost exclusively in English (perhaps with some mixed-language song) set in an urban/metropolitan context with young characters (such as *Delhi Belly*). This suggests that Hinglish works less as a strictly linguistic definition and more as a broad cultural reference to a glocalised youth culture.

The Hinglish turn in Hindi cinema is viewed as a direct result of the changing conditions of exhibition and distribution, with the space made available in multiplexes for smaller-budget and more original films and the rise in cinema ticket prices that has made cinema-going into a largely middle-class affair (Athique 2011). A new crop of filmmakers are seeking to interpret the youth Zeitgest and taking advantage of this conjuncture, and a growing number of speakers recognise themselves in the language spoken in these films and in the characters and attitudes they portray.[39]

The Hinglish of films is also seen as a result of a new practice of dialogue writing in which writers write dialogues directly in Hinglish (in Roman script, I presume) instead of writing them first in English and then translating them into Hindi.[40] As Anna Vetticad (2011) points out:

> This change has come through a painful transition period of at least a decade during which characters in Bollywood films would often utter a sentence in English and immediately translate it into Hindi, clearly reflecting the filmmaker's fear that audiences would be put off by too much English. Such dialogue writing was an awkward mish-mash of tongues, very much like the titles of many films that were released in the early part of the last decade . . . 'Baaz: A Bird in Danger', 'Karz: The Burden of Truth', 'Ek Rishtaa: The Bond of Love'.[41]

The discussion around Hinglish films suggests that in the context of films Hinglish at present is playing the role of a (growing) sub-culture and niche market, while marking a deep cultural gap from Hindi-only films, the blockbusters that do well in the hinterland.[42] For example, according to Vetticad, Prakash Jha's 2010 film *Raajneeti* was a blockbuster:

> but was still ridiculed for a sequence in which everyday Hindi was suddenly replaced by a more old-world variety in just one conversation, with words like 'kintu', 'parantu' and 'jyesht putra' thrown in, seemingly to remind us that the film was based on the Mahabharat.[43]

'Hinglish titles: empty coffers?' titles one newspaper article, reporting that:

> Hinglish may be the order of the day in Bollywood, be it the film titles, lyrics or even dialogues. But while the films seem to have found takers in multiplex audience, barring a few films most apparently fail to strike a chord with the single screen theatre-goers and smaller towns. 'In the smaller centres, people often find it hard to grasp the language. So catchy titles or lyrics may work for their catchy tunes, the dialogues often fail to make the impact they would with the multiplex audiences,' says a leading distributor. (Naval-Shetye 2011)

Thus, rather than a unifying effect, Hinglish in cinema seems rather to mark the *limits* of its social and cultural inclusion, with the limited popularity and communicability of Hinglish films beyond the metropolitan multiplexes revealing the culturally and spatially stratified nature of Hinglish and its exclusions.

Together with advertising, film songs are the other domain in which the creativity and aesthetics of Hinglish have been discussed. Creative director (his catchline '*Thanda Matlab Coca-Cola*' (Cold drink means Coca Cola), won him the 2003 Cannes Lion Award at the Cannes Lions International Advertising Festival) and film lyricist Prasoon Joshi is the most vocal supporter of the creative potential of Hinglish in film songs:

> You must have heard the song *Masti ki pathshala* from the film *Rang De Basanti*. It has a line that says: '*Talli hoke girne se, samjhi hamne* gravity . . . ' Now this line has the English *gravity*, Punjabi *talli*, Hindi *samjhi*. Which language is the song set in? It expresses a youth's experience . . . How does a language become potent? For one, you can express nuances, the grey shades . . . (Joshi, in Kothari & Snell 2011:194–5)

It is notable that Hindi film songs have long been praised for the musical and linguistic range and eclecticism, and English phrases and words have been used in film songs – to humorous effect – since at least the 1940s (Vohra 2014; Ravikant 2014). But what Prasoon Joshi is pointing towards is the ability of contemporary Hinglish songs to engage in wordplay and word creation and to express the emotional world of contemporary metropolitan youth. In the same vein others have praised the Hinglish songs of films like *Dev D* or *Delhi Belly* for their inventive rejection of cloying romance, thus encapsulating the new emotional landscape of the post-liberalisation generation:

> The phrase 'Emotional Atyaachar', from the song of the same name written by Bhattacharya for the movie *Dev D*, has now passed into the vocabulary of a generation that, for the first time, is learning to deal with modern Americanized notions of love and lust in an Indian context.[44]

Since then, *Emotional Atyachaar* (Emotional Torture) has become the title of a programme on the youth-oriented TV channel Bindass that has adapted the US format of *Cheaters*.[45]

What about Indian television? This is a fluid and fast-changing field, with channels and production houses diving for new trends and scrapping programmes that attract few viewers. Beyond the important field of news programmes and channels, currently the main genres of Indian television consist of soap operas, mythological serials, and reality shows. Hinglish appears prominently in youth-oriented serials on Channel [V] (Parmar 2014) and in reality shows, whereas mythological and family-oriented soap operas like those of Ekta Kapoor's production house use only Hindi (Munshi 2010).

In the first two episodes of Channel [V]'s dating show *Dare 2 Date,* which ran for two seasons between 2009 and 2011, young participants – either college students or college dropouts – began speaking in English in their self-presentation or when they first met, but then mixed or switched between English and Hindi, particularly when one perceived that the other's English competence was limited. Hindi-only sentences were definitely marked and, particularly when voiced by the UK-born anchor Andy, used parodically, for example to invoke the cultural expectation of a 'beautiful love story' ('*ek larki thi anjani si, ek larka divana-sa, aur unke bich hui ek manohar prem kahani*' Once there was an innocent girl, and a lover boy, and they both fell in love) only to reject it ('*is show men aisa khuch nahin hoga*!' There'll be nothing like that on this show!).[46]

In the first episode, 18-year-old middle-class Malvika, about to go to college, dates 22-year-old Delhi-urban-village Jat boy Kash, cash-rich but English-poor (Andy calls him a *desi* prince). Malvika introduces herself to the camera first in English 'Hi, I'm Malvika, I'm 18 years old', then switches briefly to Hindi before going back to English '*Mainne apna school abhi khatam kara*' (I have just finished *school*), using the colloquial Delhi perfective *kara* instead of *kiya* 'and I am looking out for college', and keeps an informal conversational style switching back and forth when talking about her favourite colour pink, '*Jo bhi pink dikh jae mujhe chahiye*' (Whatever I see in pink I must have it) and her dreams to meet a Prince Charming. Kash introduces himself wholly in Hindi, with a strong Haryanvi accent, and the only English words and phrases he uses in his self-introduction are '*real estate*' and '*we are farmers*'. When he first meets Malvika accompanied by his trail of cars and an armed guard, she is impressed. 'He's wearing pink, my favourite colour ... I like his style, is the car his?' and begins speaking in English. When he replies to her in Hindi and she realises his limited competence she quickly switches to Hindi until she *wants* to underline their socio-cultural difference:

M: So what do you do right now?
K: Fashion designer.
M: Fashion designing? [cut]
K: *Ap kya karte hain din bhar*? (What do you do all day?)
M: Well, I've just finished school now, I'm preparing to go to college.
K: Schoolgirl, ah.
M: I finished school, *to ab main* college journalism *ke lie ja rahi hun.* (*I finished school*, so now I am going to college to do *journalism.*)
K: *Patrakaar banna chahte hain*? (You want to become a journalist?)
M: *Patrakaar*? (Journalist?) [cut; they discuss the future, what to do ahead]
K: *Age barhne ki socha*? ... *Bahut sare prastaav hain* ... *Chunao laro,* fashion *laro, sundarta hai aapke lie.* (Have you thought about moving ahead? ... There are many offers ... Fight for elections, fight for *fashion*, you have beauty.)
M: *Kya karun,* elections? Elections, *kis chiz ke*? (What should I do, *elections*? *Elections*, of what?)
K: *Sansad* (Parliament) ... [M is incredulous; cut]
M: Excuse me, we don't belong to the class that owns farmhouses and ... We are all creative people. My mother's an artist, my father's an architect. *Aisi* lifestyle *nahin hai.* (We don't have that lifestyle.)
K: *Chalo chalo chalo. Apke papa kya,* building *banate hain*? (Never mind, never mind. Does your papa make *buildings*?)

M: Architects.
K: Building *banate hain.* (They make *buildings.*)
M: Well, if that's what you call it.
K: *Karvaenge kabhi kaam unse.* (I'll make him work for me sometime.)

When the programme cuts to her comments to the camera on this first meeting, it is interesting that language is how she chooses to express their socio-cultural differences:

> He's not bad, he's a decent-looking guy. *Par jo apna munh kholte hain to* we can run away. *Matlab ki kya bolte hain wo khud hi samajh sakta, aur koi samajh nahin sakta.* (But as soon as he opens his mouth, *we can run away.* I mean, he's the only one who can understand what he's saying, no one else can.)

Though they *look* compatible and inhabit the same metropolitan youth space of Delhi, wear similar kinds of clothes, and embrace similar consumer aspirations (fancy cars, fancy restaurants with champagne), their social and cultural values are very different (needless to say, she finds him very old-fashioned) and the way they speak and hear the other's speech is a precise index of their difference. Though they both understand each other in either Hindi, English or a mix of the two, they have different ranges of competence. When they *want* to be inclusive, this combination of languages allows them to do so, but they can equally use language to underscore their differences, as Malvika does. It is not only what Kash says (or does not say), his accent and the way he speaks immediately locate him in a particular class. Hinglish strives to include but still indexes class and cultural difference.

Conclusion

Despite the earlier colonial history of English and Hindi language mixing (Trivedi 2011), English and Hindi language ideologies in postcolonial India both resisted and snubbed mixing. Yet in the last two decades ideas of language purity have lost ground, and both Indian English and Hinglish, whether with a Hindi or an English matrix, have acquired public recognition and become symbols of the new upwardly-mobile, ambitious, and confident India in advertising and the media. Tellingly, in public discourse *both* are often called Hinglish. Hinglish then covers a range of phenomena, from Hindi with many English loanwords, actual switching, English with many Hindi words, and Indian English. And while claims over rights and entitlements continue to pitch the case for Hindi against English, a modicum of Hindi-English bilingualism is part of the everyday life and repertoire of a large and growing percentage of the population, even those with a very limited grasp of the English language.

Yet triumphalistic calls for Hinglish as the language of the future and as a unifying force not only downplay the limits of its social (and spatial) inclusion and the social and class stratification that language still indexes, they also ignore other processes at work, such as the parallel growth of Hindi as a language of politics and news and the limited bilingualism and language shift that attend to English-medium education. For this reason it is useful to disaggregate the domains of language use and investigate the extent, role, meaning and acceptance of language mixing, and to note the tones and accents that accompany its use (unmarked, marked, parodic, informal, etc), the role of mixing within the particular speaker's linguistic repertoire, and the listeners' reactions. More broadly, it will be necessary to study the social reach and variations of Hinglish in terms of speakers' age, background, location, and lifestyle, and to go beyond the ebullient discussions in the media, before we can have anything resembling a complete picture.

Acknowledgements

I would like to thank Aida-Mihaela Arosoaie for her web-research work, and the British Academy International Partnership for funding to conduct research in India in partnership with Ravikant at SARAI/CSDS, Delhi, Rajend Mesthrie and the anonymous reviewer for constructive criticism.

Funding

This was supported by a British Academy International Partnership with SARAI/CSDS, New Delhi [grant number PM120032].

Notes

1. In India the phenomenon is of course not limited to Hindi but is common in other Indian languages, alongside combinations of Hindi with other languages (Mokashi-Punekar 2011; Prasad 2011). For Taglish as the moniker for English-Tagalog-Spanish mixing in the Philippines, see Rafael 1995.
2. I broadly follow Peter Auer's (1998) use of the terms code-mixing and mixed language.
3. 'Is Hinglish a single force? Just *one* idea?' muses advertising guru and commentator Santosh Desai. 'Or is it a combination of several ideas – a word that captures multitudes of different strands or strategies ... ? Are there different intentions at work there?' (Desai, in Kothari & Snell 2011:203).
4. As CEO of FM Radio Mirchi Prashant Panday puts it in rather stark terms, 'Since 1991, when liberalization happened, economic policy and progress started to dismantle the caste system – the age-old system where your occupation was pre-decided by the caste and place you were born in. Today, development has become much more egalitarian – which strata you come doesn't matter. As long as you have the right skill set and the right attitude, you can join any sector' (Panday, in Kothari & Snell 2011:193).
5. Documented examples range from Rudyard Kipling (Sharma 2011), Urdu poet Akbar Ilahabadi (Nijhavan 2010:269–71), Phanishwar Renu's 1954 Hindi novel *Maila Anchal* (Hansen 1981), and of course Salman Rushdie's *Midnight's Children* (savagely dismissed in Trivedi 2003 and more judiciously analysed in Srivastava 2005).
6. Reactions in Hindi media were mixed: some positive (Saini 2011), but most were critical, for example 'Hindi par phahraya, Hinglish ka parcham' (Hinglish's flag flown over Hindi) *Ranchi Express* 14 April 2012 <http://ranchiexpress.com/158227> (accessed 31 January 2015).
7. The bibliography is vast, from Kachru (1975 & 1978), Malhotra (1980), to Dey & Fung (2014).

8. For example Viswamohan (2004), Mesthrie (2005), Bhatt (2008), Si (2011); for useful methodologies Androutsopoulos (2012) and Sebba (2012).
9. This is the approach fruitfully taken by the Kothari & Snell (2011) volume, still the only one available.
10. Thus Anuja Chauhan's Pepsi ad '*Yeh Dil Maange More!*' (1998) was used as a title for a 2004 Hindi romantic comedy film (*Mahadevan*) – and sued for breach of copyright; it had earlier been adopted as a personal motto by Indian Army captain Vikram Batra, who was killed in 1999 during the Kargil war and posthumously awarded India's highest military honour; in the 2014 election campaign, Sonia Gandhi and Narendra Modi sparred over the latter's use of the phrase in an election speech in Batra's home town; see Ghosh (2014).
11. As the example of 'Mera *number* kab aayega?' (When will my turn come?) below shows: 'number' is a long-attested loanword in Hindi, but in the 2007 Pepsi ad, it was re-accented as part of aspirational Hinglish; it was re-accented again as the name of a call-in show on Star TV in 2011, where number meant phone number while referencing the popular ad.
12. Witness the debate over the entrance test to Civil Service (UPSC) exams: in the television debate *We The People*, NDVT host Barkha Dutt consistently slotted positions that differed from a plain espousal of English as Hindi *and* anti-English, despite the fact that the speakers (Ashok Vajpeyi, Alok Rai and Abhay Kumar Dube) repeatedly pointed out that they were not anti-English but wanted English-educated to also be tested for proficiency in Indian languages; see <http://www.ndtv.com/video/player/we-the-people/watch-the-language-debate-hindi-hain-hum/330772> (accessed 30 January 2015).
13. As *Times of India* director Rahul Kansal put it, 'Hindi had mass appeal but no brand' (in Kothari & Snell 2011:206).
14. See Chad Nilep '"Code-switching" in Socio-cultural Linguistics' <https://www.google.co.za/#q=nilep+2006+code-switching>.
15. Ashok Chakravarty, creative head of leading ad agency Publicis India. His colleague and executive creative director, Sanjay Sipahimalani, points out that the stock of Hindi is now high in the copyrighting business: 'Ten years ago if somebody used Hindi in an otherwise perfect English sentence, I don't think we would have hired him. It would be a sign of lack of education. Now, it's a huge asset'; both quoted in Beeson (2012).
16. I am grateful to the anonymous reviewer for pushing me to articulate these features.
17. *Oye* is a Punjabi exclamation and *Bubbly* puns the English term for sparkling with the common Punjabi diminutive Babli.
18. Personal communication, New Delhi (28 August 2014).
19. See <http://www.youtube.com/watch?v=Aog_A-lqla4&feature=related> (accessed 24 July 2014).
20. See <http://www.youtube.com/watch?v=WMzZfzzG80s&feature=related> (accessed 24 July 2014). All the children wear Sachin Tendulkar masks, and at the end behind one of them is the real Sachin Tendulkar.
21. As journalist P Sainath remarks, 'For the media leaders, the lives of ordinary people make no sense in their economic calculations, they cannot buy the products that these guys are selling'. Nero's Guests <http://www.youtube.com/watch?v=4q6m5NgrCJs> (accessed 17 March 2012).
22. Former Bihar chief minister Laloo Prasad Yadav famously did not care about criticism from English-language journalists but wanted his photo taken: as he put it, his readers could not read English newspapers but could see his photograph printed.
23. See also Rohit Prakash's presentation 'Remix ke daur men Hindi' (Hindi in the time of remix) at the SOAS/SARAI Hinglish workshop in New Delhi <http://sarai.net/hinglish-workshop-18-19-august-2014-recordings/> (accessed 30 January 2015).
24. 'The politicians arguing about the Reservation for Women Bill in parliament swing back and forth between English and whatever language channel they may be giving a sound bite to.

"Let me tell you," they declare, "*iska koi* easy solution *nahin hai*!" (Let me tell you, there is no easy solution to this issue)' (Mohan 2010).

25. See his speech on YouTube <http://www.youtube.com/watch?v=t3UC8fJ5nl0> (accessed 23 July 2014).
26. See <http://www.youtube.com/watch?v=TIiRIoyjf5Y&feature=relmfu> (accessed 23 July 2014).
27. See interview on *Walk the Talk* <https://www.youtube.com/watch?v=1iNUEB7B5do> (accessed 23 July 2014).
28. Apoorvanand, 'Language strategies in political speech', SARAI Hinglish workshop <http://sarai.net/hinglish-workshop-18-19-august-2014-recordings/> (accessed on 20 January 2015).
29. See references cited in note 8 above.
30. As documented in many newspaper articles such as Kumar (2014). He notes that these are 'coaching classes, most of which offer two to three-month crash courses in spoken English'. Interestingly, not only those from vernacular-medium schools, but also some from English-medium ones are enrolling themselves in such classes. Explaining the trend, Kishore Kumar Banerjee, director of British India, says, 'With premier management institutes like IIM-Ranchi, BIT-Mesra, etc, bringing students from metros with a fluency in English, local students are realizing the need to hone their communicative skills to survive competition'. Ganguly-Scrase and Scrase (2009) record urban middle-class anxieties in Kolkata that the older pride in the Bengali language has jeopardised professional opportunities for the young generation.
31. See Prashant Panday the workplace today 'has become much more egalitarian – which strata you come doesn't matter. As long as you have the right skill set and the right attitude, you can join any sector' (see note 4 above).
32. 'Hinglish, for them helps to break the "formal" environment at office, and makes the boring dull office conversations more peppy and spiced-up. "An usual day at my office is all about work, work and more work, and added to that the late hours . . . it all can make life really miserable. So, we all colleagues try to keep the office environment as stress-free as possible, and conversing in a language that's fun, youthful and absolutely *hatke*, like Hinglish, does help a great deal,' proclaims engineer, Amit Sharma; Sujata Chowdhury (2008).
33. 'Hinglish, a strict no no in BPOs!', Nofil, *Indian Express* 13 May 2010 <http://www.hindustantimes.com/india-news/hinglish-a-strict-no-no-in-bpos/article1-542998.aspx> (accessed 31 January 2015).
34. As Nandini Gooptu (2013:11) puts it: 'Urban areas have witnessed a hitherto unprecedented proliferation of private hospitals, educational institutions, leisure and entertainment venues, hotels and hospitality units, large scale organized retail outlets and shopping malls. Maintenance, cleaning, catering and house-keeping in such mass private property, as well as the protection, safety and security of such spaces and their owners and users, have led to both an immense surge in demand for suitably trained labour and a radical transformation in the nature of work at the bottom of the urban formal sector.'
35. Nandini Gooptu, personal communication (25 July 2012).
36. As Krishna Kumar puts it, 'The Hindi-medium schoolchild very quickly understands that the sources of his/her knowledge are a translation whose original text is in English; e.g. arithmetics and science, where the terminology is so artificial that one needs to know the English word in order to understand the Hindi one. S/he is socialised in a world of knowledge that is full of disparities/unbalances and which produces a lack of self-confidence.' Whereas 'the English-medium schoolchild perceives a harmonious world of knowledge and acquires self-confidence through praise and social respect. After the first pain of translations his/her world becomes a wide, international world (even in her actual means are limited), whereas the world of the Hindi-medium child will shrink and s/he will cover up that limited world with the "cover" (*jhalar*) of nationalism' (2001, my translation). For a recent study, see LaDousa (2014), also Ramanathan (2005).

37. For example, 'Teachers of almost all the subjects, save languages, deliver their lectures in a mixture of Hindi and English, so that students coming from different backgrounds might easily comprehend them' (Mishra 2011).
38. See, for example, Kothari & Snell (2011:194); but see also Tripathi's alarmist newspaper article (2003): 'Excessive use of "Hinglish" from an early age is now being linked with speech disorders like stammering and "faulty production of sound" among children. Unable to articulate well, because of "faulty" bilingual usages, the children end up in a situation where they are neither versed in English, nor in their own mother tongue.'
39. 'Says trade analyst Amod Mehra, Entertainment Network, "Today, middle-class and poor people have virtually stopped going to the theatres, thanks to the spiralling prices of the tickets. Hence, the main audience for the film is the educated and the upwardly mobile urbanite. These people relate to Hinglish films better because this is exactly what they speak – a bit of Hindi and a bit of English. Besides, they relate to the characters in Hinglish films strongly; they find the larger-than-life image of characters in the candy-floss and action films too unrealistic"' (Lalwani 2003).
40. See Anna Vetticad (2011), 'There's something about the way language is being used in Bollywood these days. Characters in many major films now speak Hindi the way Indians do in real life – formally in formal situations, casually among friends, melding it with our mother tongues if our roots don't lie in the Hindi belt, and injecting English into our speech whether we are public-school-educated-city-bred folk or street urchins in small towns whose accents are a product of repeated interactions with foreign tourists. A number of Bollywood writers these days are working hard to ensure that the Hindi their characters speak is not textbook-ish or unreal; equally important, that their Hindi dialogues are not direct translations of English sentences; and that their English dialogues don't reek of Western serials and films.'
41. She argues that such self-translation is now 'incongrous': 'it's so incongruous when Amitabh Bachchan in Jha's 2011 release "Aarakshan" more than once treats viewers to a direct English translation of a dialogue he's just delivered in Hindi – "*Kya aap mujh par jaativaad ka aarop laga rahe hain*?" followed by "Are you accusing me of being casteist?"' (Vetticad 2011).
42. Actor-turned-director Deepak Tijori makes the interesting observation that censors are less strict for Hinglish films – clearly reflecting their differential role vis-à-vis the urban middle class and the urban and rural poor (quoted in Lalwani 2003).
43. Writes Trisha Gupta (2011): 'As a young woman who writes screenplays and dialogue for Bollywood recently informed me, people "in real life" no longer say things like "*Kya waqt hua hai?*" or "*Tum yahan kaise?*" The idea of speaking full sentences in Hindi is now so anachronistic as to be automatically funny.' This is obviously a metropolitan view that does not reflect practices outside Mumbai and Delhi and a limited social group.
44. '[Amitabh] Bhattacharya takes Hinglish seriously as a language, and treats it with respect. For him, it's less a medium to elicit laughs by some clever juxtapositioning of Hindi words and English ones, but more a hybrid language that nails contemporary reality ... The new wave of lyric writers like Jaideep Sahni and Bhattacharya are at the forefront of these successful experiments with Hinglish, which has liberated the Hindi film lyric, allowing the film song to widen its ambit a wee bit; it can now talk about things other than eternal love and cloying romance. Even when the subject is as hackneyed as love, it is now approached in a more direct manner, like in the lyrics of "Jaa Chudail", also from Delhi Belly, where a disgruntled lover spits out the following, "*Ungli pe nachake tune/ Chuna jo lagaya mujhe/ Arey jaa jaa jaa/* Go to hell ... */Arey jaa ja ja/* I want silence/ *Jaa chudail, Jaa chudail*"' (Mehrotra n.d.).
45. See videos on the official Youtube channels <https://www.youtube.com/show/emotionalatyachaar> (accessed 23 July 2014).
46. He then switches to mixing and switching '*Kya kar paaenge, ek dusre ko* impress, uh*?* So let's find out! *Aj kaun jaaega* date *pe?*' (Will they be able to *impress* each other, uh? So let's find

out? Who will go on a date today?) <https://www.youtube.com/watch?v=0hbOysIorv0> (accessed 23 July 2013).

References

Androutsopoulos, J. 2012. 'Repertoires, Characters and Scenes: Sociolinguistic Difference in Turkish-German Comedy'. *Multilingua* 31:301–26.

Athique, A. 2011. 'From Cinema Hall to Multiplex: A Public History'. *South Asian Popular Culture* 9(2):147–60.

Auer, P. 1998. 'From Code-switching via Language Mixing to Fused Lects: Toward a Dynamic Topology of Bilingual Speech'. *InLiSt* 6:1–30.

Baldauf, S. 2004. 'A Hindi-English Jumble, Spoken by 350 Million'. *The Christian Science Monitor* 23 November <http://www.csmonitor.com/2004/1123/p01s03-wosc.html> (accessed 3 September 2012).

Beeson, M. 2012. 'Hinglish Copywriting' <http://www.buzzwords.ltd.uk/Hinglish-copywriting.pdf> (accessed 3 September 2012).

Bhatt, R. 2008. 'In Other Words: Language Mixing, Identity Representations, and Third Space'. *Journal of Sociolinguistics* 12(2):177–200.

Chauhan, A. 2008. *The Zoya Factor*. New Delhi: HarperCollins.

Chowdhury, S. 2008. '"HINGLISH" – is apna cuppa chai!!' *Blogspot* <http://sujatachowdhury.blogspot.co.uk/2008/01/hinglish-is-apna-cuppa-chai.html> (accessed 5 September 2012).

Desai, S. 2010. 'Advertising is Widening the Gap between Haves and Have-nots'. Blog *City city bang bang* 21 April <http://santoshdesai.com/2010/04/advertising-is-widening-the-gap-between-haves-and-have-nots/> (accessed 3 September 2012).

Dey, A. & Fung, P. 2014. 'A Hindi-English Code-switching Corpus', in N. Calzolari, Kh. Choukri, T. Declerck, H. Loftsson, B. Maegaard, J. Mariani, A. Moreno, J. Odijk & S. Piperidis (eds), *Proceedings of the Ninth International Conference on Language Resources and Evaluation '14*. ELRA 2410–13.

Dube, A.K. 2014. 'Final Discussion. SARAI Hinglish Workshop, 18–19 August' <http://sarai.net/hinglish-workshop-18-19-august-2014-recordings/> (accessed 31 January 2015).

Ganguly-Scrase, R. & Scrase, T.J. 2009. *Globalisation and the Middle Classes in India: The Social and Cultural Impact of Neoliberal Reforms*. London: Routledge.

Ghosh, D. 2014. 'Yeh Dil Maange More: Sonia Gandhi vs Narendra Modi over Martyr's Words'. *NDTV* 5 May <http://www.ndtv.com/elections-news/yeh-dil-maange-more-sonia-gandhi-vs-narendra-modi-over-martyrs-words-560189> (accessed 30 January 2015).

Gooptu, N. 2013. 'Servile Sentinels of the City: Private Security Guards, Organized Informality and Labour in Interactive Services in Globalized India'. *International Review of Social History* 58(1):9–38.

Gupta, T. 2011. 'Does "Hinglish" Democratise English, or Bastardise Hindi?' [first of a two-part piece on Hinglish] Blog *First Post* 29 June <http://trishagupta.blogspot.co.uk/2011/07/does-hinglish-democratise-english-or.html> (accessed 4 September 2012).

Hansen, K. 1981. 'Renu's Regionalism: Language and Form'. *The Journal of Asian Studies* 40(1):273–94.

Jaikrishan, R. 2011. 'Gungho with Hinglish'. 1 August <http://www.gla.org.in/news_detail.php?id=30> (accessed 2 September 2012).

Jeffrey, R. 2000. *India's Newspaper Revolution: Capitalism, Politics and the Indian-language Press, 1977–1999*. London: Hurst.

John, B.K. 2007. *Entry from Backside Only: Hazaar Fundas of Indian English*. New Delhi: Penguin India.

Kachru, B. 1975. 'Toward Structuring the Form and Function of Code-mixing: An Indian Perspective'. *Studies in the Linguistic Sciences* 5(1):74–92.

Kachru, B. 1978. 'Code-mixing as a Communicative Strategy in India', in J. Alatis (ed), *International Dimensions of Bilingual Education*. Washington, DC: Georgetown University Press.

Khanna, P. 2010. 'The Most Hilarious Ads Ever …'. *Hindustan Times* 6 February <http://www.hindustantimes.com/television/the-most-hilarious-ads-ever/article1-505890.aspx> (accessed 30 January 2015).

Kidwai, A. 2014. 'The Linguistics and Politics of Mixed Codes: Understanding Site and Manner'. SARAI Hinglish Workshop, New Delhi <http://sarai.net/hinglish-workshop-18-19-august-2014-recordings/> (accessed 31 January 2015).

Kothari, R. & Snell, R. (eds). 2011. *Chutneyfying English: The Phenomenon of Hinglish*. New Delhi: Penguin.

Krishnamurthy, M. 2011. 'Furtive Tongues: Language Politics in the Indian Call Centre', in R. Kothari & R. Snell (eds) *Chutneyfying English*. New Delhi: Penguin.

Kumar, K. 2001. 'Language and Social Division', in R. Agnihotri & S. Kumar (eds), *Bhāṣā, bolī aur samāj*. Delhi: Deshkal Prakashan.

Kumar, K. 2014. 'Ranchi takes the English Route to Achieve Success'. *Times of India* (Ranchi edition) 18 July <http://timesofindia.indiatimes.com/city/ranchi/Ranchi-takes-the-English-route-to-achieve-success/articleshow/38596813.cms> (accessed 23 July 2014).

LaDousa, C. 2014. *Hindi is Our Ground, English is Our Sky: Education, Language, and Social Class in Contemporary India*. New York: Berghahn Books.

Lalwani, V. 2003. 'Hinglish, the New Catchphrase in Bombay' <http://www.rediff.com/movies/2003/jan/06list.htm> (accessed 5 September 2012).

Malhotra, S. 1980. 'Hindi–English, Code-switching and Language Choice in Urban, Upper-middle-class Indian Families'. *Kansas Working Papers in Linguistics* 5:39–46. <http://kuscholarworks.ku.edu/bitstream/handle/1808/544/ling.wp.v5.n2.paper3.pdf?sequence=1> (accessed 13 May 2015).

Mehrotra, P.K. n.d. 'Run DK Run: Dirty Lyrics that Ring Perfectly True'. Blog *First Post* <http://m.firstpost.com/ideas/run-dk-run-dirty-lyrics-that-ring-perfectly-true-34040.html?page=3> (accessed 4 September 2012).

Mesthrie, R. 2005. 'Assessing Representations of South African Indian English in Writing: An Application of Variation Theory'. *Language Variation and Change* 17:303–26.

Mishra, B.K. 2011. 'Hinglish in Vogue in PU [Patna University]'. *Times of India* 12 June <http://articles.timesofindia.indiatimes.com/2011-06-12/patna/29649720_1_hinglish-language-pu-hindi> (accessed 5 September 2012).

Mohan, A. 2010. 'English or Hinglish – Does it Matter what Indian Students are Learning?' *The Guardian* Mortarboard blog <http://www.guardian.co.uk/education/mortarboard/2010/jan/27/english-hinglish-for-indian-students> (accessed 4 September 2012).

Mokashi-Punekar, R. 2011. 'Views from a Different India: Not Hinglish but Nagamese', in R. Kothari & R. Snell (eds), *Chutnefying English*. New Delhi: Penguin.

Munshi, S. 2010. *Prime Time Soap Operas on Indian Television*. New Delhi: Routledge.

Naval-Shetye, A. 2011. 'Hinglish Titles, Empty Coffers?' *DNA (Daily News & Analysis)* 8 June <http://www.dnaindia.com/entertainment/report_hinglish-titles-empty-coffers_1552531> (accessed 5 September 2012).

Nijhavan, S. 2010. *Nationalism in the Vernacular: Hindi, Urdu, and the Politics of Indian Freedom*. New Delhi: Permanent Black.

Ninan, S. 2007. *Headlines from the Heartland: Reinventing the Hindi Public Sphere*. New Delhi: Sage.

O'Barr, W.M. 2008. 'Advertising in India'. *Advertising and Society Review* 9(3) <http://muse.jhu.edu/journals/advertising_and_society_review/v009/9.3.o-barr.html> (accessed 3 September 2012).

Parameswaran, R. 2012. 'Moral Dilemmas of an Immoral Nation: Gender, Sexuality, and Journalism in *Page 3*' <http://ijpc.org/journal/index.php/ijpcjournal/article/viewFile/10/12> (accessed on 4 September 2012).

Parmar, S. 2014. 'Channel V Serials: The Changing Language of a Youth-oriented TV Channel'. SARAI Hinglish Workshop, New Delhi <http://sarai.net/hinglish-workshop-18-19-august-2014-recordings/> (accessed 31 January 2015).

Prasad, G.J.V. 2011. 'Tamil, Hindi, English: The New Ménage à Trois', in R. Kothari & R. Snell (eds), *Chutnefying English*. New Delhi: Penguin.

Rafael, V. 1995. 'Taglish, or the Phantom Power of the Lingua Franca'. *Public Culture* 8:101–26.

Ramalingam, K. 2009. 'Poor Parents Pushing Children into English Schools'. *India Together* 26 October <http://indiatogether.org/kgiriedn-education> (accessed on 23 July 2014).

Ramanathan, V. 2005. *The English-vernacular Divide: Postcolonial Language Politics and Practice*. Clevedon: Multilingual Matters.

Ravikant. 2014. 'Phir bhi Dil hai "Hinglishtani"? Historicising the Contemporary'. SARAI Hinglish Workshop, New Delhi <http://sarai.net/hinglish-workshop-18-19-august-2014-recordings/> (accessed 31 January 2015).

Roy, N. 2004. 'What's "Veni, Vidi, Vici" in Hinglish?' *Business Standard India* 19 October <http://www.businessstandard.in/india/news/what%60s-%60veni-vidi-vici%60-in-hinglish/191117/&> (accessed 2 September 2012).

Saini, N. 2011. 'Film, Adworld or TV par Vah! Hinglish Bolie (Say "Hinglish, Great!" in films, the ad world and TV)'. *India Today* 20 December <http://aajtak.intoday.in/story/english-mix-hindi-rocks-in-add-world-1-687692.html> (accessed 31 January 2015).

Sebba, M.M. 2012. 'Researching and Theorising Multilingual Texts', in M.M. Sebba (ed), *Language Mixing and Code-switching in Writing: Approaches to Mixed-language Written Discourse.* New York: Routledge.

Sharma, D. 2011. 'Return of the Native: Hindi in British English', in R. Kothari & R. Snell (eds), *Chutnefying English.* New Delhi: Penguin.

Si, A. 2011. 'A Diachronic Investigation of Hindi-English Code-switching, Using Bollywood Scripts'. *International Journal of Bilingualism* 15(4):388–407.

Snell, R. 1990. 'The Hidden Hand: English Lexis, Syntax and Idiom as Determinants of Modern Hindi Usage'. *South Asia Research* 10(1):53–68.

Srivastava, N. 2005. 'Languages of the Nation in Salman Rushdie's *Midnight's Children* and Vikram Seth's *A Suitable Boy*'. *ARIEL: A Review of International English Literature* 36(1/2):207–31.

Tripathi, A. 2003. 'Expert Links Hinglish with Poor Articulation'. *Times of India* (Lucknow edition) 7 December <http://articles.timesofindia.indiatimes.com/2003-12-07/lucknow/27212523_1_hinglish-mother-tongue-language> (accessed 5 September 2012).

Trivedi, H. 2003. 'Salman the Funtoosh: Magic Bilingualism in *Midnight's Children*', in M. Mukherjee (ed), *Rushdie's 'Midnight's Children': A Book of Readings.* Delhi: Pencraft International.

Trivedi, H. 2011. 'Foreword', in R. Kothari & R. Snell (eds), *Chutneyfying English.* New Delhi: Penguin.

Upadhya, C. & Vasavi, A.R. (eds). 2008. *In an Outpost of the Global Economy: Work and Workers in India's Information Technology Industry.* New Delhi: Routledge.

Vetticad, A.M.M. 2011. 'Mere Film ki Language'. *Indian Express* 28 August <http://newindianexpress.com/entertainment/hindi/article308535.ece> (accessed 5 September 2012).

Viswamohan, A. 2004. 'Code-mixing with a Difference: A Look at Popular Journalism in India'. *English Today* 20(3):34–6.

Vohra, P. 2014. 'Hinglish in Film Songs'. SARAI Hinglish Workshop, New Delhi <http://sarai.net/hinglish-workshop-18-19-august-2014-recordings/> (accessed 31 January 2015).

'A State of Affairs which is Essentially Indefinite': The Linguistic Survey of India (1894–1927)

Javed Majeed

King's College London

Historians of colonial India have argued that cartography was central to colonial power in India; maps came to define the British empire's authority in the subcontinent. The effectiveness of imperial geography made India a concrete entity for both British colonialists and Indian nationalists, for whom India came to be a single and coherent geographical entity whose boundaries coincided with those of the subcontinent. This article argues that the geographical imagining of India in the Linguistic Survey of India (1894–1927) was in conflict with these colonial and nationalist mappings of India. It complicated the notion of India as a single, coherent, self-referential geography, and in doing so it centralised India in a global linguistic geography. Its cartographical exercises were at odds with the colonial state's investment in a particular geographical image of India, and with the canonical nationalist geographical imagining of India as a multilingual entity as expressed in the Report of the State Reorganization Commission of 1955.

Historians of colonial India have argued that cartography was central to colonial power in India; maps came to define the British Empire's authority in India. Imperial cartography made India a concrete entity for British colonialists and for Indian nationalists; both held India to be a single and coherent geographical entity whose boundaries coincided with those of the subcontinent (Edney 1997:2, 15–16). This article argues that the geographical imagining of India in the Linguistic Survey of India (conducted by the British colonial state from 1894 to 1927; hereafter LSI) was in conflict with these colonial and nationalist mappings of India. It complicated the notion of India as a single, coherent, self-referential geography, and in doing so it centralised India in a global linguistic geography. Its cartographical exercises were at odds with the colonial state's investment in a particular geographical image of India, and with the canonical nationalist geographical imagining of India as a multilingual entity as expressed in the Report of the State Reorganization Commission of 1955.

The Linguistic Survey's Cartographic Sensibility

Both Manu Goswami (2004) and Matthew Edney (1997) have stressed the importance of the discrete spatial partitioning of territory with no porous boundaries to the visual device of the map. The LSI, on the other hand, drew explicit attention to the fictiveness of drawing boundaries in linguistic maps. It focuses on the difficulties of fixing boundaries between languages, and therefore between the 'internal-domestic' of India and the 'external-foreign' to it. This is clear from both the published volumes and the unpublished files of the Survey.

Discussing the boundaries of Indian languages, LSI superintendent, George Abraham Grierson (1851–1941), stresses:

> Indian languages gradually merge into each other and are not separated by hard and fast boundary lines. When such boundaries are spoken of, or are shown on the map, they must always be understood as conventional methods of showing definitely a state of things which is in its essence indefinite. It must be remembered that on each side of the conventional line there is a border tract of greater or less extent, the language of which may be classed at will with one or other. Here we often find that two different observers report different conditions as existing in one and the same area, and both may be right. (1927:30–1)

This passage sets the tone for the LSI as a whole with regard to boundaries: the same volume describes the boundary between Awadhi and Bagheli as 'uncertain' and asserts that it is 'impossible to draw any clear dividing line between' between Punjābī and its neighbouring dialects (Grierson 1927:158, 168).

Another volume is also explicit about the problems of drawing boundaries between languages:

> What is wanted is definite information regarding a state of affairs which is essentially indefinite, a want which it is manifestly impossible to supply. It is most nearly supplied by selecting fixed points, where, at each, we are certain that a well-defined language is spoken, and, taking these as the foundations of our hypothesis, by drawing arbitrary lines showing the imaginary boundaries which do not exist, but which give the needed definite impression of the approximate area in which each recognised form of speech is spoken. On this principle, the maps illustrating the relative position of the various languages which form the Eastern Group of Indo-Aryan vernaculars have been drawn up, and they should be accepted subject to the above explanation. (Grierson 1903a:3–4)

The same volume describes the boundaries on maps as 'essentially indefinite', and the boundary between Bengali and Oriya as 'not capable of accurate definition', adding that in 'the boundary tract it is often difficult, or impossible to say whether a man is speaking dialectic Bengali, or dialectic Oriya' (Grierson 1903a:12). This sense of the indefiniteness of boundaries extends to other volumes. To give just two examples, Grierson writes of having 'roughly put the boundary' between Punjābī and 'Lahndā' [Siraiki], emphasising that any boundary between the two languages is approximate and a 'purely arbitrary' convention (Grierson 1916:607–8) and he speaks of the boundaries between Pashto and other languages as 'very ill-defined' (Grierson 1919a:507).

In his correspondence Grierson is equally emphatic: 'It is really impossible to say geographically where Punjābī ends and Lahndā begins' (Grierson 1919b). In the context of discussing the difficulty of classifying border dialects he refers to having to draw 'a rough line' (Grierson 1902a), but he also makes it clear in his correspondence that this roughness applies not just to border dialects. In a letter of 22 January 1902, he states:

> Of course to talk of boundary lines at all is really absurd, for languages are not divided by a sharp line, but merge into each other, and if, for the sake of definiteness, we do put down boundary lines, the language for a considerable distance on each side must be of a very indefinite character, and people will always differ as to where, exactly, the lines should be put on a map. (Grierson 1902b)

Many more examples of this geographical language exist in the LSI's volumes and correspondence. A number of conclusions can be drawn from this style of geographical imagining. While the LSI volumes reproduce many maps, Grierson goes out of his way to point to the difficulty, even the absurdity, of drawing boundary lines between languages on maps. The printed text of the LSI casts doubts on the maps it reproduces to illustrate the boundaries between languages; it foregrounds the indefiniteness which maps cannot capture. Referring to his map of where Bengali, Oriya and Bihari meet, Grierson adds that the map 'shows, so far as a map can show by definite lines, a state of affairs which is essentially indefinite' (Grierson 1903a:106). In another instance he appends to his map of the Naga group of the Tibeto-Burman family of languages the comment 'Boundaries, even where given, are only approximate', and on the map of the languages and dialects of the Bodo group in the same volume he states: 'Boundaries are only approximate' (Grierson 1903b:maps facing 1 & 193). In other cases, he spells out why data has had to be left off a map 'for the sake of clearness', as with the case of not showing Nagpuria speakers in five districts (Grierson 1903c:166, and see map facing 140). The LSI is geographically and cartographically self-reflexive, and even as it uses maps, it frames these critically.

Edney has discussed how the colonial state's commitment to a cartographic ideal played a central role to British approaches in knowing India. This ideal was grounded in an acceptance of maps as unproblematic and truthful statements of geographical reality: 'the cartographic ideal requires that we assume that maps necessarily refer to the physical landscape and that their history is the history of their ever-increasing accuracy and comprehensiveness' (Edney 1997:23). However, as he argues, in actual fact the British mapping of India proceeded in a crisis-ridden and almost anarchic manner. From the outset, though, the LSI does not subscribe to this cartographic ideal; if anything it hollows it out by dramatising it.

As seen above, at times there is sometimes a slippage between the difficulties in identifying the boundaries of a language, to identifying languages/dialects themselves especially in border tracts (Grierson 1927:30–1). The LSI is not so much about fixing languages through classification, but about classifying them provisionally, just as it maps them provisionally. The open-ended nature of the LSI's geographical approach parallels the way it foregrounds questions which it makes clear cannot always be definitively answered (Majeed 2011). Whereas the cartographic ideal of the colonial state reflected its belief in being able to know India with some certainty, the cartography and geographical imagining of the LSI reflected a different kind of epistemological style, one that is more open-ended, provisional, and conscious about the limits of knowledge (Majeed 2011).

The LSI evokes alternative visual devices to the drawing of boundaries on a map, such as that of colours shading into each other. This is clear from the following passage:

> It would be more correct but less convenient to say that, while the language spoken at Dibrugarh in North-East Assam is extremely different, on the one hand, from that spoken at Tanda in Fyzabad, and, on the other hand, from that spoken in Jaipur in Vizagapatam, each of these shades off so continuously, yet so imperceptibly into the other two, that it is impossible to say where it begins or ends. At twenty miles from Dibrugarh, the change both to Bihari and to Oriya has, although imperceptible, already commenced . . . An ideal map of the Aryan languages of India would therefore present to the eye a number of colours shading off into each other. (Grierson 1903a:3)

Others, too, refer to shades rather than boundaries in their correspondence with Grierson. In August 1904 HW Orange, the director general of education in India, wrote to ask Grierson for advice 'with the construction of school books in India in conformity with the right linguistic principles', adding that one of the difficulties was the 'shading of one language into another and the absence of any precise geographical limit within which one standard language is spoken' (Orange 1904). For Grierson, 'shading' is the key term he uses to visualise the language map of India. In the introductory volume he envisages India as:

> An unbroken chain of dialects, all imperceptibly shading off into each other, across India to the Arabian Sea, and thence northwards through Gujarati into Sindhi, but leaping across Lahnda, into the Dardic country of the Indus Kohistan. (Grierson 1927:141)

The language of shading, then, extends to cover the whole of India as a linguistic region but it is also used in more specific instances, as for example of Halabi which 'shades off' into Oriya (Grierson 1927:614). Some of Grierson's correspondents supplement this vocabulary of shading with references to melting, referring to how Hindi 'melts into' Oriya (Assistant Director 1887). Grierson also uses images of waves and tides to depict the merging together of languages, as when he considers Lahndā/Siraiki and Punjābī, where he uses the terminology of waves and tides to convey the sense of the spreading and merging of languages ('as the tide progressed westward from its starting point, it gradually lost its body and force . . .) (Grierson 1916:614). In other instances he uses the imagery of overflowing languages, referring to how Kashmiri has 'overflowed the Pir Pantsal range into the Jammu province of the State' (Grierson 1919a:233).

The diction of shading, and the supplementary vocabulary of waves, tides, and overflowing, is in stark contrast to the images used in geographical education in English schools during the period 1870 to 1944. These images enabled pupils and the public at large to visualise both the condition and potential of overseas empire – the 'red bits on the map' were a potent symbol clearly demarcating the British Empire from other colonial empires and territories (Ploszajska 1999). The language of shading in the LSI in which boundaries bleed, as it were, as opposed to visually arresting blocks of colour with clear boundary lines, is a different way of conceptualising the world from that in imperial geography textbooks at the time.

Goswami (2004) has shown how colonial and then nationalist cartography defined the 'internal-domestic' and 'external-foreign' of India. The LSI, on the other hand, frequently breaches the boundaries between what is external and internal to India. An obvious example is the 'Map of Eastern Europe and Western Asia illustrating Aryan Migration into India' of Volume 1, which goes up to the borders of France, and includes Italy, Austria and parts of Germany (Grierson 1927:95). Linkages and connections within other families of languages transcend the boundaries of India; in the same volume, we are led from a discussion of the Munda influence on the Himalayan Tibeto-Burmese dialects to central India, Assam, the languages of Indonesia and Polynesia, and finally to the Easter Island. These 'Austric' languages, like the Indo-European family of languages, stretch almost half way across the globe, emanating, as it were, from India in the LSI's cartographic imagination (Grierson 1927:15). The imperatives of the LSI sometimes required recourse to languages outside India too; thus Grierson justifies the inclusion of non-Indian languages in his Comparative Vocabulary for the sake of comparison in the case of Indo-Chinese (Grierson 1918c) and seeks out Korean words for similar reasons (Grierson n.d.). This leads to an acknowledgement of the proliferating nature of comparativism centred on India, as when Grierson signals his wish to insert Basque words into his Comparative Vocabulary but excludes Finnish: 'I must stop somewhere' (Grierson 1920).

Furthermore, Grierson makes frequent cross-continental comparisons to highlight the size and importance of India as a linguistic entity. Bihar is compared to Yugoslavia, and the number of its speakers to the combined population of Norway and Sweden; the number of speakers of Rajasthani is half the population of England and Wales; the total number of speakers of Indo-European languages in India is more than half the estimated population of Europe; and the total number of speakers whose languages are surveyed corresponds to three-quarters of the entire population of Europe. Further comparisons in this vein include the speakers of the Austric languages being equal to the population of Denmark, those of Tibeto-Burmese languages to half the population of Switzerland, and the speakers of all Indo-European languages in India are equal to the combined population of the United Kingdom, Norway, Sweden, Denmark, Germany, Austria, France, Spain, Italy and Greece (Grierson 1927:146, 170, 28). This recurring rhetoric of numerical equivalence between different areas of the globe directs attention towards India's pre-eminence as a linguistic entity. The assertion of India's linguistic importance takes place in other contexts: in his negotiations about the word limit for his articles on Indian languages for the *Encylopaedia Britannica*, Grierson pointedly refers to how the Indo-Aryan languages in India can be compared to the Romance languages in terms of importance, and as such, should be given the same space as the latter (Grierson 1906b). These intercontinental comparisons are a form of what Sara Suleri called the 'colonial sublime' (Suleri 1992) but they also perform another function: they create a global Indiacentric geography in which attention is directed outside India in order to refocus it on India again. This is again in sharp contrast to the historical geographies of empire written between 1887 and 1925, edited by CP Lucas and then his successor HB George. The latter's *Historical Geography of the British Empire* (1904) is organised on the basis of the status of each section of empire, beginning with the British Isles, then moving to Malta, Gibraltar, Cyprus, Singapore and the Falkland Islands, and then the 'daughter nations' (Canada, Australia, New Zealand), followed by the 'dependencies' India and the West Indies, and lastly the protectorates and British dominions in Africa (Butlin 1995).

In the LSI's geographical imagination, then, a departure from India serves to magnify rather than marginalise it. This is also the case with the mapping of 'Gipsy' languages (explored in detail in Volume 11) where the LSI outlines how the 'Gipsies of Europe and their congeners of Armenia and Syria found their way to their present abodes from India, which they left from the North-West' (Grierson 1927:109). Another interesting example of this departure and then return to India occurs in Grierson's letter on the entries for 'Romany' and 'Basque' in the 1911 Indian Census:

> How on earth did 59 Romani-chals get back to India? As for the entry of Basques, I suppose it is due to the perfervid patriotism of some Spanish or French family. I hope they are in the South of India, where they can compare their mother tongues with Dravidian! (Grierson 1913)

Here kindred languages return to India in order to reconnect with it in a kind of linguistic homecoming.

For the LSI, the 'enormous dialectal continuum' (Masica 1993:25) that is India cannot be contained by the internal versus external distinction of British imperial mapping and its later nationalist incarnations. When reflecting on the possibility of drawing boundaries between languages, Grierson notes (as cited above):

> It must be remembered that on each side of the conventional line there is a border tract of greater or less extent, the language of which may be classed at will with one or other. Here we often find that two different observers report different conditions as existing in one and the same area, and both may be right. (Grierson 1927:30–1)

Other examples of this include the boundary between Bengali and Oriya, which is 'not capable of accurate definition', and so 'on each side of the border line . . . there is a mixed dialect which may be styled either bad Bengali or bad Oriya'

(Grierson 1903a:12). The LSI's mapping exercise therefore strives to accommodate different vantage points, thereby precluding reductive notions of geographical 'truth'. Edney (1997:95) has observed that the colonial state's cartographic ideal could not be implemented; no matter how accurately or precisely the world's structure is measured, that structure, he points out, is created through the surveyor's and geographer's experiential perception which is personal. The LSI, as we have seen, does not subscribe to the colonial state's cartographic ideal; in addition, it hints at shifting geographies dependent on the location and perspective of the observer and cartographer. Whereas imperial cartography defined boundaries in order to centralise the British Isles in a global imperial geography, the LSI's geographical sensibility questioned the possibility of clear-cut boundaries in order to globalise India. Its flexible and provisional cartographic sensibility centres India as a linguistic entity in the globe. Its provisional geographical epistemology secured India's pre-eminence globally, whereas for the former a cartographic ideal of one-to-one correspondence safeguarded an image of imperial pre-eminence. Something of this notion of India's global linguistic prominence is also conveyed in Grierson's endorsement of RL Turner's application for the Boden Chair of Sanskrit at Oxford:

> In his hands, Sanskrit is no longer an isolated subject of study, or one which is to be associated only with languages of the west. It occupies its proper place, both as a subject of independent study, and also as a link connecting the great languages of Europe with those now spoken in India. (Grierson 1926)

The Survey's Literary Geography

There is another way in which the LSI distances itself from the cartographic ideal of the colonial state. Edney (1997:333) has argued that the Great Trignometrical Survey (GTS) in India replaced India's physical geographic structure of mountains, plains, rivers and deserts with the abstract and mathematical geographic structure of triangles. In this respect as a genre of writing the LSI's 'geographics' forms another interesting contrast (for literary geography see Hones 2008). Each section of the Survey's volumes outlines the areas where a language or dialect is spoken. These passages are characterised by two features: firstly, their style, rather than suggesting a geographer's separation from the landscape he surveys, suggests its opposite, namely his immersion in it as he travels through it; secondly, Grierson calls attention to India's physical geography in different ways, thereby distancing himself from the abstractions that characterised other cartographical exercises such as the GTS. For example, when describing the geographical distribution of the Kuki-Chin group of the Tibeto-Burmese family of languages, he adds an orographical note describing in detail the chain of mountains rising from the plains of Eastern Bengal, about 220 miles (354.05 kilometres) north of Calcutta, stretching eastwards. The paragraphs here give elevations, the names of interlinked hill ranges and their highest points, the location of its ridges, and other topographical details (Grierson 1904:1–2). This concrete detail on India's physical landscape is replicated throughout the volumes, which far exceeds the LSI's task of classifying languages. Occasionally this takes a dubiously reductive turn, as when the features of a language are conflated with the physical landscape: when outlining the geographical territories where Pashto is spoken, Grierson adds 'The rugged character of the sounds suits the nature of its speakers and of the mountains that form their home' (1927:105–6). At other points, he refers to the mismatch between the name of the language and its actual physical extent, as in the case of Punjābī (Grierson 1916:608).

The LSI's literary geography works in other ways too. At times Grierson writes in the style of a route march, travelling through the landscape, speaking in the present continuous tense. To give two brief examples from Volume 4, he writes 'Proceeding beyond the southern frontier of the district of Chanda we reach the territories of His Highness the Nizam' and 'Proceeding from Bastar towards the west we find Maria and Gondi spoken in Chanda' (Grierson 1906a:546, 535). At other times he uses the present tense; referring to Bengali he writes:

> Its western boundary runs through the District of Singhbhum, and includes the whole of the District of Manbhum. It then meets the hill country of the Santal Parganas in which languages belonging to the alien Munda family are spoken, and is forced in a north-easterly direction up to the River Ganges which it crosses near Rajmahal. Thence it runs nearly due north, following closely the course of the Mahananda (Mahanadi of the maps) River, through the Districts of Malda and Purnea, up to the Nepal frontier. (Grierson 1903a:12)

Frequent passages such as these read as if they are taking readers on a journey with languages as a travelling companion, and here the surveyor is connecting with the landscape, not abstracting himself from it. A travelling point of view is evoked in other volumes too. When dealing with Lahndā/Siraikī of the Salt Range, for example, Grierson opens up a perspective on the linguistic map of the region with the phrase 'If you travel from Chakwal to Pind Dadan . . . ' (Grierson 1919a:433). When speaking of the way Indian languages shade into each other, he refers to:

> a well-known saying in this country [that] the language changes every twenty miles, and such indeed is the fact. A native of India travelling that distance from his home would be sure to have some expression, some name for a common article of everyday use, or some grammatical form, which was strange to his ears. (Grierson 1903a:3)

The LSI combines a rigorous scholarly apparatus with the process of reconnecting with the physical and linguistic landscape of India. This may also stem from Grierson moving to England in 1900, from where he wrote up the LSI and oversaw its publication. A number of his letters from 1900 to 1930 express increasingly nostalgic views for India as well as intense expressions of friendships with Indians, especially pandits and men of other upper-caste groups (for friendships with pandits see Grierson 1914, 1917a, 1925, 1928; and for expressions of nostalgia see Grierson 1918b and 1934).[1] The LSI's literary geography, then, was partly an exercise in nostalgic reconnection.

The LSI and Indian Conceptions of India

Finally, it is interesting to note how the LSI's geographical terminology uses qualified terms such as 'Further India', 'Greater India', and 'India proper' as a way of dealing with the complex linguistic geography of the subcontinent. In one letter Grierson refers to his task in this way: 'You will understand that the comparative tables I am preparing deal with nearly every language between Japan and Syria, or rather, deal with all the languages of Greater India, and with the languages of the Countries surrounding it' (Grierson 1918a). Grierson also corresponded with Indians and Europeans on the historical, cultural, linguistic, and architectural connections between India and south-east Asia that fall under the rubric of 'Greater India'. The Kern Institute in Leiden alerts Grierson to their archaeological atlas of 'pre-Muhammadan' Greater India, an atlas which resonates with Grierson's own preoccupation with the geography of ancient India[2] (Vogel 1934). Grierson was also a signatory to an appreciation of Professor FW Thomas' achievements on the latter's 70th birthday, which refers to how 'when to-day we are comparatively well-informed about the great expansion of Indian civilisation outside the borders of India, we gratefully acknowledge that this is to a very great extent due to your conscientious and never relaxing work' (Thomas 1937). Grierson's use of the term overlaps with Tagore's, whose collection *Greater India* (1921) appeared while the latter was on his journey through Bali, Java and Siam as part of his experience of 'Greater India' (Bose 2006:chapter 7). 'Greater India' was also evoked by other writers, including Nehru (1946:200–10), and was the subject of a periodical issued by the Greater India Society in the 1930s. Here I have only space to note that this use of qualified terms for 'India' is indicative of the complexity of the term 'India' in the LSI (for which, see Majeed 2011), whose aim is less to fix India on a map, than to evoke it as a multiple, multilayered entity with porous boundaries, on the basis of which it becomes a central locus in a global linguistic geography. The commitment to a particular cartographic ideal meant the colonial state tried to iron out the ambiguities of earlier British maps of the subcontinent (Edney 1997:23–5); Grierson also refers to earlier historical confusions, for example, to how the Dutch East Indies was confused with 'India proper' so that Malay and Bengali were conflated in some accounts (Grierson 1927:4). However, the LSI's qualified use of terms for India, its cartographic scepticism, the expansion of linguistic knowledge, and its awareness of the complexities of classifying languages, leads to an awareness of the ineradicable nature of ambiguity in mapping the languages of India. This ambiguity has less to do with confusion, though, and more to with the LSI's sense of epistemological complexity.

There are also overlaps between LSI's conception of India as a linguistic entity and other broadly conceived notions of India in a later period that were eventually marginalised by canonical nationalism. For example, in Shriman Narayan Agarwal's *Gandhian Constitution for Free India with a foreword by Gandhi* (1946) India is conceived of as a concatenation of numberless village communities: here India is not presented as a nation-state with clear-cut boundaries that need to be defended. The premise of this imagining of India is 'Violence logically leads to centralisation; the essence of non-violence is decentralisation' (Agarwal 1946:38, see also chapter 13). In the literary geography of the LSI and this version of a Gandhian constitution, it appears that India's power lies precisely in the lack of its clearly demarcated boundaries. The fact that one might be associated with the colonial state and the other with a variant of nationalism should not deter us from examining the overlaps between the two alongside their obvious differences.

The LSI's geographical imagination was also at odds with India's official postcolonial linguistic geography. The independent Indian state, in the aftermath of Partition, formulated a different approach to India as a polyglot entity. The State Reorganization Commission's (hereafter SRC) Report of 1955 does draw upon the LSI, sometimes treating it as if it represented objective scholarship. However, the main aim of the report is to contain the possibility of linguistic subnationalism in the aftermath of Partition (for which, see Mitchell 2009:chapter 6). For this reason it tries to eliminate linguistic uncertainty by containing clearly defined languages within administrative boundaries. It contains languages within boundaries, suppresses zones of indistinction between languages and/or dialects, and governs the complicated experiences of multilingualism, in order to make languages the basis of new administrative provinces. This went alongside reinforcing hard and fast boundaries between the internal-domestic and the external-foreign of India.[3]

Conclusion and Possibilities

The LSI, then, occupies a third space between the 'colonial' and the 'national', alongside other more nuanced notions of India which were sidelined by the imperatives of the nation-state. It was the postcolonial nation-state that sought to fix boundaries, speakers of languages, mother tongues, and the internal-domestic and external-foreign, not the 'colonial' LSI. It is worth pointing out that as a linguistic region 'India' is at odds with the post-Partition political map of the subcontinent. The Indian languages of the Indo-European family of languages are an obvious example of a group of languages that do not fit the political boundaries of the subcontinent, while languages such as Punjābī and Bengali that are geographically contiguous with each other span across the political borders of the subcontinent. Other languages that are not geographically contiguous are also related in families that span political boundaries. Brahui, spoken in the highlands of Baluchistan and contiguous parts of Sind in present-day Pakistan, with speakers in contiguous parts of Iran and Afghanistan, is related to the Dravidian language family of South India. This language, described as 'the most-interest exciting of the languages of the Dravidian family' (Emeneau 1980:315), is a good example of how linguistic maps do not fit well with postcolonial political maps. India as a linguistic region does not fit with India and Pakistan as political entities created out of competing nationalisms.

Historians have rightly cautioned us against 'methodological nationalism' (Goswami 2004) and have argued for the need to bring back into the historical picture multiple and alternative meanings of 'nation' that have fallen by the wayside (Kapila 2007; Bose 2007). We also have to consider multiple and potentially productive meanings of the term 'India' in what might conventionally be called 'colonial discourse' that have been marginalised by the way the nation-states of the subcontinent were ultimately defined, without ipso facto dismissing these as 'colonialist'. Ironically, the flexibly conceived geography of the LSI, and its expansively and productively ambiguous use of the term 'India', may be more in keeping with India's 'great cosmopolitan past' (Pollock 2006:575) than current nationalist ideologies. The LSI was concerned with how speakers of languages moved across the land masses of India and beyond, and as such its flexibly conceived geography can also accommodate diasporic languages and their histories in wider expanses of the globe (such as the India Ocean World), far better than the SRC's linguistic geography; indeed Rajend Mesthrie has drawn upon Grierson in discussing what he calls 'languages in indenture' in South Africa (1992:79–81). The LSI files evince other connections with the African continent. Thus, the files include a 'Memorandum on the Desirability of a Survey of Languages in Africa' of the British and Foreign Bible Society[4] which begins, in very Grierson-like fashion:

> How many languages and dialects are spoken there [the African continent] it is impossible to say: it depends partly upon what is meant by 'language' and what by 'dialect'. It would be possible to write down the names of a thousand forms of speech labeled 'languages' and a far larger number of 'dialects', without any pretence at exhaustiveness. (BFBS 1937)

The idea of a survey of languages in Africa is clearly inspired by the LSI. One of the other files also evinces an engagement with the field of African linguistics; Grierson's brief correspondence with Northcote W Thomas in May 1922 discusses the question of whether the system of representing tones in 'Oriental' languages could also be applied to tones in African languages; the question is raised as to whether current definitions of tones fit 'African facts' or not, and reference is made to research on musical tones in the Congo and the need to give the Philological Society an account of this research, with a view to 'evolve a satisfactory scheme of general application' (Grierson 1922). Thus, there are hints in the files of attempts at sharing expertise across the linguistic regions of India and the African continent. For other African linguists in the colonial period, such as Wilhelm Heinrich Immanuel Bleek, Indo-European comparative philology was a key intellectual context in which they operated, shaping their own sense of their linguistic projects (Gilmour 2006:chapter 5). Grierson also refers to how the inadequate state of knowledge of African and Indian languages in the 1870s allowed 'an impudent imposition' in Terentieff's *Russia and England in Central Asia* (1876) where the author supposedly reproduces a version of the Lord's Prayer in the language of the Hindu Kush tribes, but this version was in fact in the language of the 'Xosa Kaffirs' of South Africa – Volume 8, Part II of the LSI was to give 'genuine' specimens of the Hindu Kush languages to counter this (Grierson 1917b).

The LSI's globalised geography of India in the late 19th and early 20th centuries can be read alongside another geography of India in this period: that of the Indian subcontinent becoming the nodal point of a sub-imperial system from which peoples, ideas, goods, and institutions radiated outwards in the India Ocean world, knitting together South Africa, central and eastern Africa, the Arabian and Gulf coasts, and the Malayan peninsula, to Calcutta, Bombay and Madras (Metcalf 2007). Taken together, these land-based and maritime geographies evoke 'India' as the name for a powerfully globalised space, that (it could be argued) was later marginalised in the period of the 1930s to 1980s as India looked inward and cut itself off from the world market economy (Metcalf 2007:220–1).

This flexibly conceived space of India can also interleave with a more flexible conception of the term 'African' as argued for by Gwyn Campbell (2010). Building on the LSI we can open up the term 'Indian' alongside the term 'African' to think both outside and alongside the methodological nationalism that continues to dominate our fields, truncating our fields of vision (see also Ho 2006 on the moral map of diasporic geography being at odds with the 'bundling' and 're-bundling' of the world into nation-states). Another way to do this is also to open up to further examination colonial and postcolonial states' overlapping and differing approaches to the uncertainties of linguistic mapping in both regions, and to reconsider the extent to which the fashioning of names on maps did (or more importantly from the perspective of this article) did not imbue regions with the illusory aura of ethnographic and political certainty (see Worby 1994:392 for colonial Zimbabwe) as well as linguistic certainty.

Notes

1. These expressions of friendship are explored further in my monograph under preparation.
2. For reasons of space, I am not able to discuss this further here.
3. See the 1955 *Report of the State Reorganization Commission*, Government of India Press.
4. I do not have the space in this article to address Grierson's connection with this Society.

References

Agarwal, S.N. 1946. *Gandhian Constitution for Free India. Foreword by Mahatma Gandhi.* Allahabad: Kitabistan.

Assistant Director of Schools, Chota Nagpur Division Ranchi. 1887. 'Letter to G.A. Grierson, 13.10.1887'. British Library, Oriental and India Office Collection, European manuscripts, EUR 223/300.

Bose, S. 2006. *A Hundred Horizons. The Indian Ocean in the Age of Global Empire*. Cambridge, MA & London: Harvard University Press.

Bose, S. 2007. 'The Spirit and Form of an Ethical Polity: A Meditation on Aurobindo's Thought'. *An Intellectual History for India, Modern Intellectual History* 4(1):129–44.

British and Foreign Bible Society (BFBS) 1937 (27 October). *Memorandum on the Desirability of a Survey of Languages in Africa, Written by E.W. Smith at the request of the Editorial Sub-Committee*. British Library, Oriental and India Office Collection, European manuscripts, EUR 223/219.

Butlin, R.A. 1995. 'Historical Geographies of the British Empire, c. 1887–1925', in M. Bell, R. Butlin & M. Heffernan (eds), *Geography and Imperialism 1820–1940*. Manchester: Manchester University Press.

Campbell, G. 2010. 'The Role of Africa in the Emergence of the "Indian Ocean World" Global Economy', in P. Gupta, I. Hofmeyer & M. Pearson (eds), *Eyes Across the Water. Navigating the Indian Ocean*. Pretoria: Unisa Press.

Edney, M.H. 1997. *Mapping an Empire. The Geographical Construction of British India, 1765–1843*. Chicago: University of Chicago Press.

Emeneau, M.B. 1980. *Language and Linguistic Area. Selected and Introduced by Anwar S. Dil*. Stanford: Stanford University Press.

Gilmour, R. 2006. *Grammars of Colonialism. Representing Languages in Colonial South Africa*. Houndmills: Palgrave Macmillan.

Goswami, M. 2004. *Producing India. From Colonial Economy to National Space*. Chicago: University of Chicago Press.

Grierson, G.A. n.d. 'Letter to Revd. Mark H. Trollope'. British Library, Oriental and India Office Collection, Linguistic Survey files, S/1/1/15.

Grierson, G.A. 1902a. 'Letter to the Provincial Superintendent of Bengal, 19.5.02'. British Library, Oriental and India Office Collection, Linguistic Survey files, S/1/14/3.

Grierson, G.A. 1902b. 'Letter to Superintendent of Census Operations, NWP and Oudh, 22.1. 1902'. British Library, Oriental and India Office Collection, Linguistic Survey files, S/1/14/5.

Grierson, G.A. 1903a. *Linguistic Survey of India. Indo-Aryan Family. Eastern Group. Specimens of the Bengali and Assamese Languages. Volume 5, Part I*. Calcutta: Office of the Superintendent, Government Printing, India.

Grierson, G.A. 1903b. *Linguistic Survey of India. Tibeto-Burman Family. Volume 3, Part II. Specimens of the Bodo, Naga, and Kachin Groups*. Calcutta: Office of the Superintendent, Government Printing House, India.

Grierson, G.A. 1903c. *Linguistic Survey of India. Indo-Aryan Family, Eastern Group. Specimens of the Bihari and Oriya Languages. Volume 5, Part II*. Calcutta: Office of the Superintendent, Government Printing House, India.

Grierson, G.A. 1904. *Linguistic Survey of India. Tibeto-Burman Family. Specimens of the Kuki-Chin and Burma Groups. Volume 3, Part III*. Calcutta: Office of the Superintendent, Government Printing, India.

Grierson, G.A. 1906a. *Linguistic Survey of India. Munda and Dravidian Languages. Volume 4*. Calcutta: Office of the Superintendent of Government Printing.

Grierson, G.A. 1906b. 'Letter to Hugh Chisholm, 30.6.06'. British Library, Oriental and India Office Collection, European manuscripts, EUR 223/237.

Grierson, G.A. 1913. 'Letter to the Superintendent of the 1911 Census, 4.1.1913'. British Library, Oriental and India Office Collection, Linguistic Survey files, S/1/14/1.

Grierson, G.A. 1914. 'Letter to K.P. Jayaswal, 11.3.1914'. British Library, Oriental and India Office Collection, European manuscripts, EUR 223/265.

Grierson, G.A. 1916. *Linguistic Survey of India. Indo-Aryan Family Central Group. Specimens of Western Hindi and Panjabi. Volume 9, Part I*. Calcutta: Superintendent Government Printing, India.

Grierson, G.A. 1917a. 'Letter to L.S.S. O'Malley, 28.12.17'. British Library, Oriental and India Office Collection, European manuscripts, EUR 223/211.

Grierson, G.A. 1917b. 'Letter to F.H. Brown, 11.05.1917'. British Library, Oriental and India Office Collection, European manuscripts, EUR 223/220.

Grierson, G.A. 1918a. 'Letter to L. Milne, 20.3.1918'. British Library, Oriental and India Office Collection, Linguistic Survey files, S/1/1/15.

Grierson, G.A. 1918b. 'Letter to Edward Gait, 24.6.1918'. British Library, Oriental and India Office Collection, European manuscripts, EUR 223/238.
Grierson, G.A. 1918c. 'Letter to Director De L'Ecole Française d'Etrême-Orient, 12.08.1918'. British Library, Oriental and India Office Collection, Linguistic Survey files, S/1/1/15.
Grierson, G.A. 1919a. *Linguistic Survey of India. Specimens of the Dardic or Pisacha Languages (Including Kashmiri). Volume 8, Part II.* Calcutta: Superintendent Government Printing, India.
Grierson, G.A. 1919b. 'Letter to A.C. Woolner, 14.03.1919'. British Library, Oriental and India Office Collection, European manuscripts, EUR 223/306.
Grierson, G.A. 1920. 'Letter to W.J. Edmonton Scott, 11.03.1920'. British Library, Oriental and India Office Collection, Linguistic Survey files, S/1/1/15.
Grierson, G.A. 1922. 'Letter to Northcote W. Thomas, 14.05. 1922'. British Library, Oriental and India Office Collection, Linguistic Survey files, S/1/1/16.
Grierson, G.A. 1925. 'Letter to Maulvi Syed Abbas Husain, 4.09.1925'. British Library, Oriental and India Office Collection, European manuscripts, EUR 223/246.
Grierson, G.A. 1926. 'Letter to R.L. Turner, 11.12. 1926'. British Library, Oriental and India Office Collection, European manuscripts, EUR 223/332.
Grierson, G.A. 1928. 'Grierson to Pandit Nityananda Sastri, 12.11. 1928'. British Library, Oriental and India Office Collection, European manuscripts, EUR 223/269.
Grierson, G.A. 1927. *Linguistic Survey of India. Volume 1, Part 1: Introductory.* Calcutta: Government of India.
Grierson, G.A. 1934. 'Letter to H.H. the Maharajahdhiraja of Darbhanga, 24.01.1934'. British Library, Oriental and India Office Collection, European manuscripts, EUR 223/231.
Ho, E. 2006. *The Graves of Tarim. Genealogy and Mobility across the Indian Ocean.* Berkeley & London: University of California Press.
Hones, S. 2008. 'Text as it Happens: Literary Geography'. *Geography Compass* 2(5):1301–17.
Kapila, S. 2007. 'Preface'. *An Intellectual History for India, Modern Intellectual History* 4(1):1–6.
Majeed, J. 2011. 'What's in a (Proper) Name? Particulars, Individuals, and Authorship in the Linguistic Survey of India and Colonial Scholarship', in D. Ali & I. Sengupta (eds), *Knowledge Production, Pedagogy, and Institutions in Colonial India.* New York: Palgrave.
Mesthrie, R. 1992. *Language in Indenture. A Sociolinguistic History of Bhojpuri-Hindi in South Africa.* Johannesburg: Witwatersrand University Press.
Metcalf, T.R. 2007. *Imperial Connections. India in the Indian Ocean Arena, 1860–1920.* Berkeley: University of California Press.
Mitchell, L. 2009. *Language, Emotion, and Politics in South India. The Makings of a Mother Tongue.* Bloomington: Indiana University Press.
Nehru, J. [1946] 1989. *The Discovery of India.* Delhi: Oxford University Press.
Masica, C.P. 1993. *The Indo-Aryan Languages.* Cambridge: Cambridge University Press.
Orange, H.W. 1904. 'Letter to G.A. Grierson, August 1904'. British Library, Oriental and India Office Collection, Linguistic Survey files, S/1/2/10.
Ploszajska, T. 1999. *Geographical Education, Empire and Citizenship: Geographical Teaching and Learning in English Schools, 1870–1944.* London: Historical Geography Research Group.
Pollock, S. [2006] 2011. *The Language of the Gods in the World of Men. Sanskrit, Culture, and Power in Premodern India.* Ranikhet: Permanent Black.
Suleri, S. 1992. *Rhetoric of English India.* Chicago: University of Chicago Press.
Vogel, J.Ph. 1934. 'Letter to G.A. Grierson, 4.10.1934'. British Library, Oriental and India Office Collection, European manuscripts, EUR 223/303.
Thomas, F.W. 1937. 'Letter to G.A. Grierson, 22.03.1937'. British Library, Oriental and India Office Collection, European manuscripts, EUR 223/330.
Worby, E. 1994. 'Maps, Names, and Ethnic Games: The Epistemology and Iconography of Colonial Power in Northwestern Zimbabwe'. *Journal of Southern African Studies* 20(3):371–92.

Performing History and Constructing 'Culture': Ronnie Govender's *1949* and the Romanticism of Historical Memory

Neilesh Bose

St. John's University

Though both South Asian and South African literary and cultural studies boast deep critical traditions, rarely have critics specifically focused on dramatic literature and the performative acts of Indian South Africans. Theatre – as an aesthetic genre as well as a social institution – has been remarkably under-theorised within Indian Ocean communities, even though its power in Indian South African communities and within South African history and culture has been amply documented and analysed In theatre studies of South Asia, scholars have pushed new frontiers about the studies of colonial modern theatre as well as post-independence Indian theatres, inspired by a performance-studies turn, but the push to link theatre and performance studies with Indian Ocean, and migrant, contexts has yet to fully manifest within scholarly circles. Through an examination of Ronnie Govender's play 1949, *this article argues that theatre as a medium offers the opportunity to create specific versions of history and community identity not visible in prose literature or the novel. These versions of history and community identity are analysed with reference to the broader history of South Africa as well as the manners in which Govender's history both incorporates particular aspects of earlier definitions of Indian identity in South Africa and innovates to create images of Indo-African shared spaces.*

Though both South Asian and South African literary and cultural studies boast deep critical traditions, rarely have critics specifically focused on dramatic literature and the performative acts of Indian South Africans. With a few exceptions, the focus has been on the novel, the short story and memoir (Frenkel 2010; Chetty 2002; Govinden 2008; Rastogi 2008; Kruger 2001). Theatre – as an aesthetic genre as well as a social institution – has been remarkably under-theorised within Indian Ocean communities[1] even though its power in Indian South African communities and within South African history and culture has been amply documented and analysed (Kruger 1999; Hansen 2012, 2005, 2000; Bose 2009). In theatre studies of South Asia, scholars have pushed new frontiers about the studies of colonial modern theatre as well as post-independence Indian theatres, inspired by a performance-studies turn, but the push to link theatre and performance studies with Indian Ocean, and migrant, contexts has yet to fully manifest within scholarly circles.

Performance cultures and histories within an Indian South African context offer a critical lens onto the very nature of an 'alternative' Indian modernity (Mee 2008:19; compare Dharwadker 2011:431–432) that is not only critical of the nation, but exists in some measure a part, but definitely apart, from developments in South Asia. Performance studies and theatre studies within South Asia have also nudged closer to each other, as recent studies of *devadasis* and the performance of South Asian nationalism show (Menon 2013; Soneji 2012). Not only are performance studies methodologies appearing in new studies of the under-theorised nature of South Asian performing arts, but also point toward non-national, and trans-regional aspects of performance. In a recent study of Mohandas Gandhi's printing press and the reading practices inherent in Gandhi's world in South Africa, Isabel Hofmeyr (2013) has focused understandably on the periodical and the pamphlet, but less is known about genres like the play and the performance – a form that emerged in Indian South African communities as a recognisable genre in the apartheid era that continued to serve as a surrogate public sphere in the late-apartheid and immediate post-apartheid eras (Bose 2009; Hansen 2005, 2000). In this article, I will detail one particular play by Ronnie Govender – *1949* – which details a moment in South African history, but also constructs a particular version of history and community for Indian South Africans in the post-apartheid period.

I argue that *1949* comprises a site in which a new form of memory in South Africa, that includes Africans as agents in a shared history. I will discuss this site with reference to *1949*, which condenses a series of stories about life in apartheid-era South African Indian townships and ends with a prelude to the Indian-African riots that occurred in Durban in January of that year. Through an analysis of the play, a consideration of the life of tropes of Indian 'culture' in South Africa, and an exploration of the performance text, I argue that Govender constructed a strategic notion of Indian history and 'culture' that intervenes strongly in the creation of a viable post-apartheid reservoir of memory in lieu of documented history.

A Brief History of Indians in South Africa through 1949

The history of Indians in South Africa carries forth an increasingly documented and theorised field that intersects with the history of religion, the history of the British Empire, and contemporary anthropology (Bose 2014; Hofmeyr 2013; Hansen 2012; Green 2011:208–235; Bhana & Padchai 1984). The multicultural Dutch East India Company's settlements in the Cape region from the 1650s bought and sold hundreds of slaves to work in their domains in the Cape, nearby islands, and in the Dutch East Indies. The major precedent for Indian populations in South Africa, though, derives from the abolition of slavery in 1834 and the urgent need for manual labour in the British Empire. This history began in November 1860, as two ships, the Truro and the Belvedere, brought over 600 indentured labourers to work mostly on sugar cane fields, but also in mines, hospitals, and as special servants. From the late 1860s, the first batches of 'passenger Indians' appeared in ports across South Africa, so-named as they paid their own passages, and worked as traders, lawyers and teachers. Within this group arrived Gandhi in 1893, to represent Seth Dada Abdullah, in a conflict against the plaintiff's cousin. Though such 'passengers' set up businesses and often travelled between South Africa and India in the late 19th century, the vast majority of Indians living in South Africa by the 1940s were descendants of the indentured labourers, who numbered approximately 150,000 by the end of the system in 1911. During the years from the early 1910s through the 1940s, the Indian communities in South Africa grew significantly in population and many in Natal, the province of the majority of Indians, migrated to the industrialising portions of Durban for work in manufacturing, food processing, and manual labour in the Durban municipality (Freund 1990).

In early 20th-century Durban, as African migrant labourers were crowding the urban space and living in houses often owned by Indian landlords, Indians displayed a diversity of class positions from the petty merchant, the comparatively wealthy landlord, and the urban worker. Africans had more limited options in terms of mobility, particularly in the 1940s, as Indians dominated areas such as municipal service labour, hotel and laundry work, furniture, artisanal and sugar refinery labour, whereas Africans earned lower wages in areas such as domestic service, work at the docks and in rickshaw pulling. In a relatively minor incident in which an Indian shopkeeper caught an African boy stealing from his shop, the shopkeeper allegedly hurt the child, which led to Africans en masse proceeding to attack Indians in various parts of Durban for three days of January 1949. When it ended, 142 people had died (of these 50 Indian and 87 African), over 1,800 people were injured, over 40,000 Indians were displaced and then lived in refugee camps, 47 Indian businesses burnt, and over 700 partially damaged. Many factories fired affected Indian workers who did not return to their jobs. The Durban municipality considered deducting wages of those Indian workers who did not show up to work during the riots. The mayor of Durban coordinated a relief effort and the state conducted a full-scale investigation and attempted to manage recovery for the victims, but according to apartheid policy on the government commissions and committees, no Africans and no Indians were consulted. From the reports of the government as well as popular oral histories, white South Africans had been providing Africans with weapons and also inciting Africans toward violence, whereas the police in the beginning of the riot itself did nothing to stop the conflict. Also, oral histories have produced memories of some whites, dressed in blackface, participating in the looting and violence, intending to appear as black Africans (Vahed 1997:29–34; Ramamurthi 1994:543–546).

This event occurred only two years after the historic 'Doctor's Pact' (a joint pledge of Indo-African cooperation and solidarity) between the representatives of the Natal Indian Congress, Dr Naicker and Dr Yusuf Dadoo of the Transvaal, and Dr Xuma of the African National Congress (ANC). Simultaneously, Indian anti-colonialists like Jawaharlal Nehru publicised the plight of Indians in a racially segregated South Africa in the post-war 1940s during the construction of the United Nations (Bhagavan 2010:317–324). The 1949 riots served to mark the end of a brief moment of both Indo-African cooperation as well as internationalist anti-colonialism, as South African Indian politics after 1949 abruptly left the internationalist realm and focused more on domestic affairs.

Enter Ronnie Govender

Govender has published many stories and depictions of his memories of Indian South African life during the early days of apartheid. Born in 1934 in Cato Manor, an Indian area that was demolished because of the 1950 Group Areas Act, Govender has enjoyed a highly visible career as anti-apartheid activist, playwright and writer across genres. Recipient of several South African and globally-recognised writing awards including the Commonwealth Writers Prize, Govender's writing spans the genres of theatre, memoir, prose and poetry. However, his own history and orientation as a writer emerge primarily from the theatre, as he worked in political theatre (with others he formed the Shah Theatre Academy, in 1962, a theatre company focused on Indian and Indian South African issues) since the 1960s. In 1972, he pioneered both satirical and politically motivated theatre aimed at critiquing the apartheid state with his landmark play *The Lahnee's Pleasure*, which introduced a specifically Indian South African patois into the English language. The play premiered at the South African Black Union Theatre Festival in 1972 alongside Athol Fugard's *Sizwe Bansi is Dead* and launched an ongoing career as a playwright and cultural activist in South Africa. In addition to many other plays, Govender's most well-known writing remains *At the Edge (and Other Cato Manor Stories),* a compilation of stories about Cato Manor, Govender's childhood home. Stories in *At the Edge* depict the everyday life of Indians in the mid-20th century and one of these stories contains a dramatisation of the 1949 riots. As a play, *1949* is a dramatisation of stories written over the 1980s and early 1990s and performed first in 1994. It has been performed a number of times in South Africa since that signal year of transition for audiences in Durban and throughout the country at theatre festivals. Two notable performances were in 1994, performed by Charles Pillai, and 2002, by the actress Jayloshni Naidoo.

1949 showcases four stories of Indian South African life during apartheid in the wake of the Group Areas Act of 1950, which authorised the violent removal of many Indians from their homes and placed them into areas defined by the newly minted apartheid legislation. The play[2] is written as a one-person show narrated by a young woman, Yanambal Periasamy, who is writing a bachelor's history thesis, titled 'The role of the joint family system in the prevention of the cultural disintegration of descendants of Indian indentured labourers in Cato Manor before 1958', and opens with 'The Incomplete Human Being', a story about mourners at the death of an Indian in the community, as well as life in a Tamil school, the initially mandatory school for Tamil-speaking Indians. All stories deal with some aspect of culture and Indian life: 'Lala Phanzi', about a young Indian man arrested on a bogus charge 'Sarees, Bangles, and Bees', about domestic relations between a husband and wife; and ending with the story titled '1949', which introduces an African character who was immersed in the events of the 1949 riots, just before the violence occurred.

The idea of 'culture' in the play is introduced at every register: the student and narrator, Yanambal, is aiming to understand 'cultural disintegration', presuming that Indian culture was constant and uniform, before the era of the Group Areas Act and forced removals. The first story, about a young boy, Sathie, at the funeral of a neighbour, being admonished by elders for running away from the forced 'Tamil schools', intended to inculcate Tamil language and culture into the youth of Indian South Africa. The local Tamil teacher, a Mr Thaver, replicated the Orientalist notions of linguistic purity and antiquity, by claiming that 'we, the Dravidians, were Shaivites. We were the natives of India and lived in Harappa and Mohenjodaro in the north of India until we were invaded by war-like barbarians and were pushed to the South of India. We taught the world how to count' (4). As a statement of the playwright's own biography, the boy Sathie endured two hours of torture a day as the teacher recited statements like 'In ancient Dravida everybody was equal. It didn't matter who your father was. There was no high caste and no low caste. They were so advanced that they were amongst the first to sail on the great oceans of the world' (6). The story ends with young Sathie rising against his rigid parents and Tamil school teachers, refusing to attend, and reflecting as an adult, on the 'dire warnings of cultural disintegration and he regretted not only his own halting Tamil but also that none of his children or grand-children could speak their own tongue – THE WORLD'S OLDEST LIVING LANGUAGE' (9).

Between this beginning and the end, focusing on the prelude to the 1949 riots, Govender includes two stories that document the social history of the 1950s in Cato Manor and other parts of newly Indianised apartheid Durban, chronicling both limited upward mobility amongst Indians and the cementation of 'Indianness' of the Indian radio programme on the SABC. The play then ends with a vignette about the lead-up to the riots, replete with Zulu music opening the scene, and an opening setting of an African worker and recent urban migrant. The African worker Dumisane lives in a house owned by an Indian landlord and is being treated unusually nicely by his white boss. His white boss, Osborne, treats him with traditional paternalism, but rants about Indian business owners eating up nearby real estate. Such business owners consisted of the few wealthy Indians who escaped the ravages of the Pegging Act of 1949, which was designed to keep Indians within circumscribed boundaries of the Durban municipality. The play ends with the Dumisane, observing sales of paraffin and petrol to African workers, egged on by white bosses like Osborne, feared by Indian shopkeepers, running to save Indian friends, only to be killed by African rioters. The narrator, Yanambal, utters the final line in closing: 'There was no pity, no reason in the hearts of these malleable souls, held captive by minds more savage in their cunning – the cunning on which empires have been built' (32).

Govender presents a social history as inclusive of positive Indian-African relations, with conflicts between the two groups interpreted as manufactured from the state and from white interests. This history excludes consideration of the earlier pre-apartheid periods of colonial South Africa, such as the history of Indian political activism in the 1890s and 1900s, which aimed at *sustaining* racial segregation, bolstered by a fully racialist understanding of cultural difference. This understanding was demonstrated periodically by Gandhi's well-known comments about Indian 'civilization' and African lack of it during his 21 years in South Africa, as well as demonstrated by the various activities on behalf of Gandhi and the emergent Indian organisations to protest Indians and Africans being treated as equals in the public sphere.[3] Gandhi, and his moment in history, signifies Victorian-era racism, manifested in how early Indian protests were directed not at white interests, but at Indians being treated as blacks. This component of the history of Indian South Africans is not a part of Indian history in Govender's play. Rather, culture is a part of the account – language, Tamil school, and religion – in short, all that would be enumerated by an anthropologist. The ending to the play accounts for a historical and social interaction that was simply not possible in the Gandhian moment, but rather belongs firmly in an era after generations of Indian settlement in South Africa as well as wide-spread urbanisation, industrialisation and competition between working-class Africans and Indians. What Govender introduces is a historical interpretation of the 1949 riots through the characterisation of Dumisane, Yanambal and Osborne, white, Indian and African players in a tragic drama engineered by whites and executed by Africans.

Performing History, Constructing Culture

The play was first performed in Durban in 1994, the year apartheid was dismantled, by Charles Pillai, and revived in 2002 again in Durban, performed by Jayloshni Naidoo. The play offers insights impossible to visualise in other genres – such as the novel or the memoir – as it allows for a creative understanding of memory to speak to the present as well as cement a previously inaccessible version of South African history. As the press material for the 2002 version demonstrates, the play aimed to do what had already been done for Sophiatown and District Six, areas in Johannesburg and Cape Town respectively, that were destroyed by apartheid, whereas the characters in *1949* emerge from Cato Manor, an 'Indian' area in Natal, and so offers history to those who do not have memorials within the nation.

This was not a result of either timeless antagonism with other groups (Africans) nor did it have much to do with 'India', nor did it refer to the history of racialisation in Indian communities in colonial South Africa. This sort of Indianness is defined by its difference from Africans, coloureds and Europeans, not through the racialism of the earlier periods, but by the details of a social history, defined by Tamil language, songs and by Tamil school. This sort of difference then allows for the construction of a community that both inherits the notion of Indian difference from earlier periods and invests it with anti-apartheid urgency. Recent work on post-apartheid South Africa has emphasised the construction of 'community' in black and coloured contexts, but the Indian component is notably absent, as the criteria for having a 'community' is partially to have a history.

Constructing a history in the guise of this performance must be contextualised within the broader documented history of Indian South Africans. Even though Govender resolutely constructs a history that highlights the alliances between Indians and Africans, thereby countering a history of isolated communities in conflict, he does depend on a discourse of culture that stretches back to the late 19th century, when the pages of the *Indian Opinion* or the proceedings of the early Natal Indian Congress unequivocally recommended against any political alliance with Africans (Vahed 1997; Bhana & Pachai 1984). As a cursory reading of the history of Indian political activism will show in the 1894–1914 period, the key moment that saw the rise of Gandhi, Victorian race science and racism informs each and every step of the Indian political leadership during that period. In the 1940s, after the urbanisation and industrialisation of Durban as well as the transformation of colonial South Africa into a rising power in its own right after unionisation in 1910, Indian communities became more and more integrated into South African society as a whole, planting the seeds for later alliances. The joint Indian-African alliances that arose during the decade of the 'Doctor's Pact' effectively ended with the 1949 riots. The concept of culture inputted into the history that *1949* actively produces deletes the history of culture that depends on race in the earlier period and focuses squarely on the 1940s moments of alliance. The genre of theatre gives this sort of history a life, given the absence of Indian South Africans from pre-existing historical understandings of South Africa until the post-apartheid period.

Of course, there is another definition of Indian 'culture' brewing in the early 20th century, particularly through the writings and poetry published in the *Indian Opinion*, as well as the ways of reading, as discussed in Hofmeyr's *Gandhi's Printing Press* (2013), that derive from an emergent, Indian Ocean cosmopolitanism. Poetry in the *Indian Opinion* (Bhana & Bhatt 2011) in particular focused on an Indian self and a presumed white audience and relegated Africans either to outright exclusion or to marginalia, but Govender brings the Indian and African together in a manner that reflects a history of cultural production completely overlooked by literary critics and historians of South Africa. Not exactly 'post-resistance' (see Hofmeyr 2004), the inclusion of African characters in 'Indian' plays holds a hidden history within Indian South African theatre, such as in Kriben Pillay's *Looking for Muruga*, a play about anti-apartheid activism and partially about Indo-African relationships, also written and produced in the late apartheid period. Govender's landmark *Lahnee's Pleasure*, also serves as a precedent for chronicling the social history of Indian communities in South Africa, as it entailed a detailed view into the domestic travails of Indians across the generational and economic class spectrum in apartheid-era South Africa, replete with their own particular patois and culturally specific practices most likely unknown to other South Africans.

Complicating any notion of the historical nature of Indian South Africans by inputting the long-neglected history of Indian slaves' presence in the pre-1860 slave trade does occur in the work of other writers, such as the work of Achmat Dangor (see Kruger 2011), but Govender for the first time enables an Indian actor to embody a South African history inclusive of African and Indian together. The historical potential of the piece was realised through the performance process of the lone actor, Jailoshini Naidoo, who performed the play in Cape Town, Johannesburg and Durban, as well as on tour in various parts of the world. When interviewed, Naidoo detailed how the play offers a history that was alive in her family, her community, but not recorded in any history book or taught in any school, or a part of the contemporary world of South African memorialisation. It formed an alternative history that came alive when she played the characters of Dumisane, Osborne and Yanambal, three players in the final scene of 1949, in which the white character eggs on the black character to attack Indian businesses and families. But the character of Dumisane, a young gentleman who saves the Indian family, is a part of the local social history of Ronnie Govender and comes to life through Naidoo's performance, via the inhabitation of a character of a different race, but a part of a shared history. When interviewed, Naidoo stressed how the play was both natural but difficult, as the history in the play 'was a history we [Indians] all know, but never learnt in school'.[4] The history depicted, particularly in the last portion of the play, resonated strongly with Naidoo as re-enacting that scene brought her to tears nearly every performance. One element that emerges from a textual reading of the play is the notion of Indian 'culture' – adhering to elements drawn from a familiar story – 'family values', 'work ethics', often painted in pictures of obedient, quiet, 'middleman' immigrants. As performed, 'culture' was simply meant to portray a difference produced by the state and was hardly of importance when Indians and blacks collided, as the play suggests, because of conflicts engineered by the white ruling power. As Govender the playwright remembers (given that the event is one he lived through), relationships between blacks and Indians were certainly shot through with segregation, but shared, humane and unstained by continual conflict. Naidoo's experience in rehearsals and interactions with the audiences confirms this popular history, as black and Indian audience members both commented on how the popular history of 1949 was a shared black and Indian struggle (though one that bears no documents or other recorded, 'traditional' sources of evidence). As Naidoo was performing black, white and Indian characters such a shared history came into view. Given the troubled history of recent experiences of conflict and antagonism between Indians and blacks at various points in post-apartheid history, *1949* offers an alternative history which, in Naidoo's words, 'allows the born-free [those born after 1994] generation a chance to understand a different history'.[5] In postcolonial societies, terms like 'culture' and 'history' are often manufactured from nationalist or state-level sources, or exist at myriad popular levels.[6] Though the question of history for societies like postcolonial India has been addressed, the role of history for 'exogenous others'[7] in post-settler societies like South Africa has only now begun to come into view. Before the end of apartheid, such a history simply did not exist in any book, play or other textual artefact. Africans and Indians belong to a recognisably shared history within this piece and are enacted by an Indian actor, instantiating through Indian bodies what could not be transmitted via text. Here we find an engagement with culture which yields questions about history in ways that would be improbable in metropolitan locations such as postcolonial India.

The nature of a playtext as a document of dramatic literature offers a specific vision of performance in contexts with institutional theatrical infrastructures, documented theatre histories, particular audiences, and critical discourses of theatre. For such theatre traditions, memory self-consciously refers to a canon, however defined. Govender stands in between the well-known constructions of *lieux de memoire* and the *milieux de memoire* of Pierre Nora (1989:7–25), as there was no *lieux* to create, reference, or demolish in the manner of western theatre practitioners, since memory as an actual agent and the discourse about theatre that could be confronted simply did not exist in the context of late apartheid 1990s Indian South Africa. As Govender remarked in a 1994 interview, the greatest hits of western theatre history, though appreciated as *literature*, could not be marshalled as practical guidelines for performance (Solberg 1999:149–159; Bose 2009:363–375). Therefore, *1949* cannot be seen in the long history of memory theatre, i.e. the Sam Shepards, Suzan Lori-Parks and Samuel Becketts, who in the tradition of dramatic criticism inherit modernist approaches of Ibsen, Strindberg, Miller and August Wilson (Malkin 1999; Favorini 2008). Rather, Govender works out of an empty conceptual space as he creates the history of Indian South Africans through performance, not a textual guideline or a history to counter or revise. His characters, of Dumisane and Yanambal, the narrator, are portrayed through one Indian actor, and construct in the last vignette, a history of the 1949 riots reverses ideas of Indian and African antagonism, but yet places the notion of 'Indian culture' as defined by language, tradition and religion. Govender's piece fits into Loren Kruger's categorisation of contemporary theatre as 'not yet post-apartheid but rather tentatively post-anti-apartheid' (1999:191). It is anti-apartheid in its interpretation of the 1949 riots as a conditioned state-sanctioned and white-directed action. The nature of a performance piece of this type yields the possibilities that a play with institutional funding and discursive history does not allow, as the piece itself ensures that one actor play multiple roles, countering at one level the naturalist push for each community to only represent themselves, forcing an Indian actor to play African and white roles, thereby constructing a way for difference to be represented but without verisimilitude as a criteria. Before the end of apartheid, such a history simply did not exist in any book, play or other textual artefact. Though not directly subsequent to the experiments of Gandhi and others involved with the *Indian Opinion*, Govender in his late apartheid context carries forth a tradition of destabilising any fixed notion of Indian identity simply for its own sake and so forms another portion of the evolving historiography of the multicultural and insurgent literary spaces of the edges of empires.

The site of diaspora requires conceptualisation beyond either homelands and their extensions, or the obverse of simplistic and unending localisms. Recent work on post-apartheid South Africa has emphasised the nature of 'community' in the world of artists:

> characterized by a dialectical relationship between past histories and lived experience in the present. Rather than deny history, they mobilize (and in some cases invent) historical memory as a tool for dealing with the contradictions of life in contemporary South Africa. (Coombes 2003:245)

When we input Indian experiences into the *longue duree* conception of historical memory in South Africa, we find recognisable contradictions and tools to confront those contradictions, but something more is at work here than a standard postcolonial anxiety. As Duncan Brown notes in his thorough investigation of *At the Edge*, Govender explores what it means to belong in South Africa in a manner far removed from abstract intellectual migrancy often preached in metropolitan locations, as in a context like Indian South Africa, 'the postcolonial in the "South" is primarily a matter of conditions of survival, rather than a metaphorical or allegorical space of hybrid freedom' (2005:113). In such a space as the Indian South African (specifically not the Indian of territorial India), theatre, as opposed to the novel, appears as the medium through which a community identity and an insurgent history may be authorised. As Pallavi Rastogi (2008) mentions about her analysis of South African Indian literature, fictional writings during the apartheid period stressed inclusion and belonging in South Africa, but start to shift toward new concerns after apartheid. Govender's *1949*, and the genre of theatre behind his contributions, manifests a continuity from the earlier generation's emphasis on a shared apartheid history, well into the post-apartheid years. As recent criticism of South African Indian literature demonstrates, the post-apartheid era of the present is a 'time of memory', and the particular roles of the performance and the theatrical genre, awaits a complete analysis within literary criticism.[8]

Given the complex history of linkages between India and South Africa from the early modern Indian Ocean slavery context (1652–1860), the indentured labour period (1860–1911), the period of industrialisation (1911–1945), and apartheid/post-apartheid from 1945 onward, full-scale theoretical and empirical investigation must move beyond a simplistic framework of empire or nation. Precisely because a long history betrayed by an incomplete and fragmented historiography offers a different vantage point on the past than those in colonial India or territorial South Asia, scholars must open themselves to different forms of expression and genres of cultural production that revise our notion of postcolonial literature, such as theatre and performance. Postcolonial South Asia and post-apartheid South Africa both offer intriguing possibilities for linking histories that neither simply confirm nor deny the discursive power of the nation. Ronnie Govender's

1949 offers a history that can neither be fully predicted only from the Indian nation-state's emergence in 1947 nor from the 'new' South Africa in 1994.

Notes

1. In the conclusion of *Reconsiderations*, Ronit Frenkel (2010) states that fiction has been the main object of critical attention to the neglect of other genres.
2. All page references are to the unpublished playscript (R Govender *1949*) in the author's possession.
3. One particular example is Gandhi's notorious 1896 protest against the 'invidious distinction' of shared 'native' and 'Indian' entrance to the Durban Post Office, as well as the anxiety about how laws in colonial South Africa would 'degrade the Indian to the position of the Kaffir' (*CW* 1:229).
4. Personal interview with Jailoshini Naidoo (9 September 2014).
5. Ibid.
6. See Partha Chatterjee (2002:1–18).
7. See Lorenzo Veracini (2010), as well as Neilesh Bose (2014).
8. *A Time of Memory* (Govinden 2008) explores the work of Aziz Hassim, Imraan Coovadia and Sita Gandhi as a lens into the broader contours of memory in South African Indian contexts.

References

Bhagavan, M. 2010. 'A New Hope: India, the United Nations, and the Making of the Universal Declaration of Human Rights'. *Modern Asian Studies* 44(2):311–347.

Bhana, S. and Bhatt, N.S. 2011. *A Fire that Blazed in the Ocean: Gandhi and the Poems of Satyagraha in South Africa, 1909–1911*. New Delhi: Promilla and Company.

Bhana, S. and Pachai, B. 1984. *A Documentary History of Indian South Africans*. Cape Town: David Phillip.

Bose, N. 2009. *Beyond Bollywood and Broadway: Plays from the South Asian Diaspora*. Bloomington, IN: Indiana University Press.

Bose, N. 2014. 'New Settler Colonial Histories at the Edges of Empire: "Asiatics", Settlers, and Law in Colonial South Africa'. *Journal of Colonialism and Colonial History* 15(1) <http://muse.jhu.edu/journals/journal_of_colonialism_and_colonial_history/v015/15.1.bose.html>.

Brown, D. 2005. 'Narrative, Memory, and Mapping: Ronnie Govender's At the Edge and Other Cato Manor Stories'. *Current Writing: Text and Reception in Southern Africa* 17(1):108–128.

Chatterjee, P. 2002. 'Introduction', in P. Chatterjee and A. Ghosh (eds), *History and the Present*. London: Anthem.

Chetty, R. (ed). 2002. *South African Indian Writings in English*. Durban: Madiba Publishers.

Coombes, A.E. 2003. *Visual Culture and Public Memory in a Democratic South Africa: History after Apartheid*. Durham: Duke University Press.

Dharwadker, A. 2011. 'India's Theatrical Modernity: Re-theorizing Colonial, Postcolonial, and Diasporic Formations'. *Theatre Journal* 63:431–432.

Favorini, A. 2008. *Memory in Play: From Aeschylus to Sam Shepard*. New York: Palgrave Macmillan.

Freund, B. 1990. *Insiders and Outsiders: The Indian Working Class of Durban, 1910–1990*. Porstmouth, NH: Heinemann.

Frenkel, R. 2010. *Reconsiderations: South African Indian Fiction and the Making of Race in Postcolonial Culture*. Pretoria: UNISA.

Gandhi, M. (ed). 1869–1948. *The Collected Works of Mahatma Gandhi* [*CW*] Vol 1. Delhi: Publications Division: Ministry of Information and Broadcasting, India.

Govinden, B. 2008. *A Time of Memory: Reflections on Recent South African Writings*. Durban: Solo Collective.

Green, N. 2011. *Bombay Islam: The Religious Economy of the West Indian Ocean, 1840–1915*. New York: Cambridge University Press.

Hansen, T. 2000. 'Plays, Politics, and Cultural Identity among Indians in Durban'. *Journal of Southern African Studies* 26(2):255–269.

Hansen, T. 2005. 'Melancholia of Freedom: Humour and Nostalgia among Indians in South Africa'. *Modern Drama* 48(2):297–315.

Hansen, T. 2012. *Melancholia of Freedom: Social Life in an Indian Township after Apartheid*. Princeton: Princeton University Press.

Hofmeyr, I. 2004. 'Popular Literature in Africa: Post-resistance Perspectives'. *Social Dynamics* 30(2):128–140.

Hofmeyr, I. 2013. *Gandhi's Printing Press: Experiments in Slow Reading*. Cambridge, MA: Harvard University Press.

Kruger, L. 1999. *The Drama of South Africa: Plays, Pageants, and Publics Since 1910*. New York: Routledge.

Kruger, L. 2011. 'Black Atlantics, "White Indians", and "Jews": Locations, Locutions, and Syncretic Identities in the Fiction of Achmat Dangor and Others'. *South Atlantic Quarterly* 100(1)111–143.

Malkin, J. 1999. *Memory-theater and Postmodern Drama*. Ann Arbor, MI: University of Michigan Press.

Mee, E. 2008. *Theatre of Roots: Redirecting the Modern Indian Stage*. Kolkata: Seagull.

Menon, J. 2013. *The Performance of Nationalism: India, Pakistan, and the Memory of Partition*. New York: Cambridge University Press.

Nora, P. 1989. 'Between Memory and History: *Les Lieux de Memoire*'. *Representations* 26(Spring):7–25.

Ramamurthi, T.M. 1994. 'Lessons of Durban Riots'. *Economic and Political Weekly* 29(10):543–546.

Rastogi, P. 2008. *Afrindian Fictions: Diaspora, Race, and National Desire in South Africa*. Columbus, OH: Ohio State University Press.

Solberg, R. 1999. *Alternative Theater in South Africa: Talks with Prime Movers since the 1970s*. Pietermaritzburg: Hadeda Books.

Soneji, D. 2012. *Unfinished Gestures: Devadasis, Memory, and Modernity in South India*. Chicago: University of Chicago Press.

Vahed, G. 1997. 'The Making of Indianness: Indian Politics in South Africa During the 1930s and 40s'. *Journal of Natal and Zulu History* (17):1–36.

Veracini, L. 2010. *Settler Colonialism: A Theoretical Overview*. Houndmills, Basingstoke: Palgrave McMillan.

Index